The Art of
Story
Telling

Identity Development A Sustainable
Defense Against Existential Threats

The Art of Story Telling

Identity Development A Sustainable Defense Against Existential Threats

Eric L. Johnson, PhD

CITI OF BOOKS

CITIOFBOOKS, INC.
3736 Eubank NE Suite A1
Albuquerque, NM 87111-3579
www.citiofbooks.com
Hotline: 1 (877) 389-2759
Fax: 1 (505) 930-7244

Ordering Information:
Quantity sales. Special discounts are available on quantity purchases by corporations, associations, and others. For details, contact the publisher at the address above.

Printed in the United States of America.

ISBN-13:   Softcover   979-8-90124-110-3
              eBook   979-8-90124-111-0

TABLE OF CONTENTS

INTRODUCTION

I dentity is not simply an answer to the question; who are we? It is an understanding and perspective that accounts for that and so much more that includes: Who we think we could be? What it means to be on our journey? Why we navigate challenges and moments of success the way we do? Where do we think our path leads? Are we inspired by hope or moved by despair in our decision-making process? Identity accounts for all these dynamics and more. Identity does not simply answer the question who we think we are, it often forces us to confront what we think that means to us, the people we love, and the people we understand to be threats or competitors. Of course, none of us approaches this task in the same way. As a result, the art of developing our story requires us to seek data that affirms or questions our story and/or chosen path.

On this artistic journey each of us is making decisions that work for what we believe is in the interest of the story we are living. The art is both confirmed and complicated by the reality that there are no guidelines on how we make decisions, other than ones we accept on our own terms, for our own reasons that may be rational or not. Consequently, it is incredibly difficult to provide someone with advice on a journey that you do not fully understand, particularly when understanding may not be possible.

This book attempts to aid in successful identity development by making the process itself conscious, relevant, empowering, and on-going. We move in our in own interests when we become more reflective of the stories we live and the impact they have on us, the people we care about, the goals we want to achieve, and the fears we wish to dismantle. Hopefully, a reader leaves this piece with important questions to consider about self exploration that contribute to what they believe to be a better version of themselves and leaving the world they sojourn better because they passed through. Each journey is unique, and no recipes are available but better almost always happens after good questions are addressed and accounted for by the processes, we use to navigate the paths we are choosing.

I.

WHAT IS IDENTITY DEVELOPMENT AND WHY IS IT IMPORTANT?

Identity development and its importance

I dentity development is no small matter in the existence of anything. In the case of individuals, families, organizations and nations it is the mechanism by which existence is both affirmed and assigned meaning. As an identity is developed it provides the basis and lens by which all information is gathered, analyzed, incorporated, or dismissed. It is a crucial element in forming a path forward and assessing the significance of potential threats. Threats here represent anything that constitutes a challenge or obstacle to the stories we believe we are living. In part identity development represents the assertion of a chosen path that is both arbitrary and inescapable. Every individual, family, organization or nation makes conscious decisions to determine a path that works best for them and as part of their identity they develop stories that explain their action path. While the decision to choose a path is in many ways subjective, the force that compels the decisions is not. All things that live must defend that life. Identity development is a decisive component in the defense of a chosen life.

Invariably what life means is heavily influenced by the identities we assume and the stories we use to explain them. While the identities we assume are in part malleable, subjective, and conscious, the unconscious need to develop an identity to defend seems to be destined for anything to have a sustained existence. The development of an identity is a complex process that follows no predetermined procedure or path, it is neither completely rational nor are the decisions to form it entirely conscious. That reality makes identity development both complicated and varied. The process of coming to terms with claiming a space in the world seems to be driven by a deep need to understand how one fits into the stories they we want live. Individuals, organizations, and nations all seek to not only justify their place in the world, but also to defend that place against all threats ideological, spiritual, cultural, emotional, psychological and of course existential.

Identity development is a journey that has no clear destination. Developing a sense of understanding for one's existence appears to be a sojourn that compels more questions than answers. At its essence it invites the incorporation and collaboration of irrational ideas, beliefs, hopes, dreams, fears, and failures in a way that is entirely unique to the subject. However, while the analysis and meaning of the contributing factors to its development are specific, the places we go to find information are perplexingly common. Individuals often seek to reflect on their familial backgrounds, experiences, beliefs, hopes, fears, and aspirations. The meaning of each of these shifts for a variety of reasons is an individual's lived experience. Families often assess not only the basic question of "who constitutes it?", but also "what it means to be constituted." Organizations and companies are often intensely forced to defend their existence in a world of competitors and other factors that often serve as authentic threats to their survival. Even nation-states must develop a collective psyche that serves as means of connection to different demographic groups whose perceived and actual interests can be seriously divergent.

Identity development in each of these cases is the nuts and bolts that serve as the fundamental parts necessary to assemble the reality to which we wish to respond. Identity development is many things that include both a rational and irrational response to a perceived environment and its supposed challenges. In a world inundated with a near limitless number of discern-able hazards, identity development becomes a mechanism by which jeopardy is prioritized and assessed. The development of an identity represents one's claim to a space of existence. An identity answers fundamental questions about the understanding one has about the space one occupies. As such identity development in part defines a threat, constructs acceptable responses, assesses potential resources, and authorizes action.

In every conceivable circumstance identity development serves as the first line of defense to any perceived threat, because it is the presence of identity that makes the awareness of the threat detectable. For all living things, death serves as a primary danger to be continually evaluated, and one's identity is the most effective method to detect, assess, and neutralize identified hazards. Individuals, families, organizations and nation-states all contend with the existential threats they perceive. While the context and content vary greatly, they all have the same goal. The defense of their survival as they perceive it.

Individual implications (physical, ideological, and psychological)

Few things matter more in the lived experience of humans than both surmising and exploring the distinctive characteristics that serve as the basis for one's uniqueness and individuality. The making of an identity is a process that requires consistent affirmation and/or evaluation. As such none among us truly ever completes the task. Every experience and understanding is examined through the lens of one's identity and the stories used to justify it. How one perceives the role of characteristics such as race, class, gender, sexual orientation, culture, religion, and even sex is often a function of identity. A perplexing reality is that those factors both inform our identities while simultaneously being shaped by them. Consequently, Identity development is often a complex compilation of emotional, psychological, physical, and sometimes spiritual factors one uses to construct a story that explains one's place in the world. Each of us constructs a personal narrative that explains why we occupy space in the world and how we should operate in that space. No two people ever develop the exact same narrative, even if they share the same experiences, similar physical features, and/or similar understandings of the space they occupy.

People are often confronted with the distinction between what they do and who they are. The connection between the two is often misunderstood as mutually exclusive but these questions are intimately related; to understand one is to gain some insight into the other. The quest to know thy self is one that takes a lifetime because we are often undergoing transformation and/or modification. Life is periodically but consistently sending updates to better understand why we believe we exist. Our identity is forced to both incorporate and apply learned information in way that best suits our survival and encourages the story we are telling ourselves about why we are here and the meaning of that existence.

Physical

Physical survival is in the end the ultimate aspiration and all other understandings of survival in one way or another are driven by the innate desire to exist. What it means to exist varies greatly from one identity to another and that variation frames each of our understanding of the environment in which we operate. What constitutes a risk to our perceived life? The physical aspect of survival is in part the most fundamental element to the subject of identity development; however, it is also profoundly complex. As we assess our physical identity at its most basic level, we are often assessing our physical characters as one of two things. We identify those aspects of our physical identity that we believe serve as a strength in our effort to survive and what things we perceive as potential vulnerabilities to be guarded against. While most of our identified physical features are probably some elements of each, there is a tendency to see them as one or the other.

As it relates to our size, weight, skin color, and other physical features on a rudimentary level, we are evaluating whether those characteristics support the potential longevity of our survival. However, we are also often doing much more. We are often evaluating our physical features against our hopes and aspirations and how they might help or hinder them. More importantly, privately we assign ourselves value based on the outcome of these evaluations and how they relate to our perceived existence and the stories that explain it. In that effort we are constantly calculating what operates in our interests and what we believe does not. Obvious and not so obvious features such as intelligence, attractiveness and perceived importance, each are separate factors but are often indiscriminate in the impact of one's perception and the assessment of what it means to be.

To the extent that we believe we are valued in the social construct we identify as our life, is the extent to which we psychologically find shelter within ourselves. However, there are few among us, if any, who understand that shelter to be sufficient. As a result, most of us are seeking in some way to improve our psychological standing within our own minds. We seek to make our physical experience respond to our perceived emotional, cultural, spiritual, and psychological vulnerabilities. All based on not what we observe about our physical characteristics but how we value and assess them as part of our innate desire to exist.

Not completely unlike many living things in nature, the congruence of our physical characteristics and the environment in which we operate has a direct relationship with not only our survival but more specifically to the threats we analyze and assess. As with other living things in nature, there are limited responses with near inexhaustible expressions of creativity within them. The survival options available are inextricably connected to one's physical characteristics. The ability to flee danger, hide from it, confront it, or amass allies are all profoundly impacted by physical characteristics. As such, identity development sorts through these options and gages a course of action that is perceived as the best method to promote survival. No option is without challenges and specifically unique obstacles; however, each presents a viably perceived route forward. The impact of physical characteristics on the development of an identity can't be measured with any psychological precision. However, physical characteristics not only frame the available responses to a perceived threat, but they also play a significant role in shaping the perception of the risks the threat constitutes. Identity development accounts for factors both conscious and unconscious, and nothing is more conscious than the perception of the physical space one occupies.

Ideological

The idea of what it means to exist can often be identified as the source of most ideological stands. Ideology is that aspect of story-telling that attempts to frame the world in terms and concepts that are relevant, applicable, and comprehensible. Ideology is the aspect of identity development that works to intellectually capture both areas of concern and mark areas of strength. Ideology is useful because it provides conceptual short cuts that identify threats, potential tools and or weaponry to respond. However, ideology does more than identify threats and tactics. Ideology is essential in providing the stories we are living with the reasoning and explanations for "why" the world is the way it is. Often, it is ideology that provides the conceptual framework for many important questions, such as: Why is something a threat? What does the threat mean? Why is removal or nullification of the threat justified? While these are important questions to answer about any challenge to one's existence, ideology does much more than respond to the defensive aspect of threat assessment.

Ideology also attempts to explain one's place in the world, moreover it helps to provide the reasoning and purpose for one's existence. Interestingly it not only justifies one's own existence but how that existence relates to others. It frequently indirectly attempts to address deep fears and inadequacies in existential precepts. In other words, ideology is not simply a benign effort to understand the world for the purpose of survival, although that is certainly a significant factor, ideology is frequently a structure that seeks to impose a justified superiority that is fueled by deep ceded vulnerabilities that are perceived as existential. In that way ideological aspects of identity development can be both the most impressionable and simultaneously the most treacherous. The power of ideology is in its simplicity, it's nearly impossible to defend something that is not understood or even misunderstood. Ideology provides clarity on who belongs where and why to both mitigate threats and when necessary, destroy them. Clarity is a critical element because it supplies both the devotion and drive to take action, sometimes over long periods of time, which defends against perceived threats while simultaneously reinforcing a sense of purpose and direction no matter how much it may misrepresent an objective reality. Indeed, the strength of ideology is that it only requires minimal objective verification to establish legitimacy. Ideology tends to be long on belief, hopes, fears, and agenda but is often short on objective information that does not reinforce the ideological stance. Ideology is often presented as a rational response to dangers in the perceived world, when its psychological and emotional workings necessitate features that are not entirely rational.

Psychological

The psychological makeup of any human being is first and foremost designed to aid in the overall fight to survive. Where ideology attempts to explain the world outside of us, the psychological aspect of identity development seeks to explain, govern, and justify the happenings in our own minds. Our psychological make up attempts to evaluate the world through our place in it. Moreover, our psychological make up attempts to assign value to our presence in the world but in a complicated way it also attempts to determine the value we have to ourselves. The psychological make up of any person, organization, or nation is first obligated to assist in developing a perceived internal value for existence. The psychological aspect of identity development must answer questions such as: What worth do I bring to the world I perceive? How do I believe other people assess my worth? Do I value the importance I believe I have? How do I believe the space I occupy contributes to the world I perceive? These are not simple questions to consider, and few among us reflect on them deliberately. Nonetheless continued survival is often predicated on adequate responses to questions like these and many more.

The psychological aspect of identity development provides the energy to survive. Survival has an incalculable component that is related to will and desire. The psychological aspect of identity provides the stories we tell about survival with the necessary aspiration, belief, desire, or obligation to contribute that is in some way unique, worthy, or otherwise significant in our own estimation. Aspiration provides the internal need to respond to the inevitable challenges to survival big and small, significant and trivial, simple and complex. It is difficult to defend an existence that has no reason to be. It is for that reason that the psychological aspect of identity is a vital part of the stories we are living but it is profoundly complex. It is complex because what challenges aspiration changes over time and more importantly, the appropriate response to the challenge is always unique to the subject. It is difficult to provide others with a method that works for them because it is hard to do so without a healthy understanding of what serves as their reason for survival.

The psychological aspect of identity attempts to assign value to our understanding of our worth in the world we perceive. Moreover, this evaluation process extends to our perception of how we think others calculate our value. This process is important because it impacts our evaluation of potential threats. If we are not sure of the value, we have to ourselves, then the most significant threat to our survival may be in our own heads. The actions we take and resources that we mobilize to protect ourselves and further our existence is different than it would if the threat was elsewhere in our environment. There are times when the most significant existential threat we must confront is the one in our own minds. Moreover, when we miscalculate how others assess our worth and we may be perceiving threats that are not authentic and overlooking threats that are far more hazardous. The psychological aspect of identity development should never be underestimated because too often the danger we pose to ourselves is the most significant threat any one of us faces.

Identity development considerations

The development of an identity is not compiled compartmentally, each aspect of who we think we are is interwoven into a complex amalgamation that is us and the stories we are living. The interplay of all aspects of identity (ideological, physical, psychological, and others) makes the narratives we construct that we call our lives interestingly unsophisticated and multifaceted simultaneously. It is not at all surprising that no two of us is composing the exact same story. However, we all have the exact same goal, which is why there is always much overlap and intersection.

The desire to survive is common to us all, but the how and why is a singular endeavor. The journey to understand ourselves and others begins with the notion that no two of us is identical, but we are using common information pools to determine our path. Identity development is a singular process, but it responds to a world and factors we are all required to address. An understanding of the shared need to survive and its complicating factors provides us all with more tools and weapons to protect, construct or defend the lives we create.

II.

ORGANIZATION IDENTITY
(ONTOLOGICAL AND CULTURAL)

Organization has played a central theme in the survival of the human species, that much cannot be disputed. The idea that humans can come together to share and pool resources for the expressed purpose of forging common interest and goals has served as an almost unequaled phenomenon in human development and survival. Moreover, the interplay between the stories we construct about the groups we belong to and the stories we are individually living in is never simple nor is it always rational. Humans have sought organizational arrangements in a variety of forms not always for the expressed purpose of promoting the survival of the species, some organizational arrangements are designed to respond to specific needs and interests. In such cases, humans organize as a strategy to meet necessities and demands that cannot be met simply by the efforts of single individuals. In very unique ways to the organization and individuals in them the stories used to justify individual and collective worth are both challenged and affirmed. Nonetheless they are both altered by the interaction in ways that can be both beneficial and dangerous. Complicatedly, the organizations themselves seek to claim a space in the world and their endurance requires the ability to assess danger, respond to threats, and defend the space they believe they are worthy of inhabiting even when that understanding endangers some of its members.

In short, an organization is when humans trade some of their individuality for a social structure empowered to impose and enforce arbitrary rules, regulations, customs, norms or laws in ways that are compulsory. The range of associations employed by groups of humans to reach desired ends varies greatly. The myriads of social groupings to achieve economic, political, religious, cultural or any other form of communal pursuits all mandate some subversion of individual interests for what is often perceived as a greater shared purpose. An organization in theory provides each of its members with opportunities that otherwise would not be available when left to their individual abilities and talents.

What is organizational identity?

Organizational identity development is similar to Individual identity development in that both endeavor to respond to similar challenges. Both have to recognize and classify the space they occupy and then justify why that space is worthy of existence. Where the tools available for individuals to engage in this process are often limited by a singular imagination and informed by a distinctive effort to survive.

Organizations on the other hand are strengthened by the ability to mobilize collective resources; intellectual, imaginative or otherwise to recognize, clarify, and defend the space of its concern. Organizational identity is a combination of prescribed policy and procedures, an identified mission and goals and most importantly by its actions otherwise known as organizational practice. An organizational identity is most significantly evaluated by an analysis of its stated goals and/or values compared to its practices. Organizational identity is expressed in a number of ways, from its membership, internal communication, resource allocation, and leadership development among other things.

In general, organizational identity is understood from the inside out, meaning from the view of a member. Organizational identity is the story it tells itself that explains its reason for being and the meaning of that existence. However, that should not suggest that external perceptions are not significant in both understanding organizational identity and developing it. Interestingly, like individuals an organization's identity is crucial to its survival. Organizations like all things that wish to survive are required to assess dangers both present and developing. Some organizations defend their survival through the values they use to do their business, but others put more energy into damaging and/ or destroying perceived competitors. Both methods can be effective mechanisms to aid the effort to survive. However, each approach impacts both the way an organization is perceived by others and the way an organization views itself. There is no question that every organization that wishes to survive must actively and effectively assess their operating environment, evaluate its capacity to navigate warnings, and overcome realized hazards that serve as barriers to their endurance.

Organizations that defend themselves through the values they purport to hold, evaluate their practice against a standard to which they wish to adhere. However, organizations who defend themselves by damaging or destroying the competition tend to evaluate themselves by a desired result. When an organization has clarity on its identity and the understood threats to its survival then practice becomes an expression of that effort. However, when organizations are not clear about their identity the ability to assess risk is significantly compromised. Organizational anxiety and fear masquerades as policy, practice and leadership. In such environments there is the danger of members of the organization distorting and misinterpreting organizational endurance with their individual interests. As a result, threat assessments include not simply the outside organizational landscape but also internal tensions that often result in the targeting of individuals within the established "community." Survival is then complicated by a compulsion to respond to perceived hazards inside the association and the resulting complicated collective responses to the dangers outside the organization.

Individual survival becomes a competitor of organizational survival and under such circumstances, organizational identity becomes one thing in practice and another in mission. Members of the community can feel compelled to respond to intimidations within the organization with as much urgency or sometimes even more earnestness than they do to perils outside the organization. Sometimes even conflating the two as though they were the same thing. When people, particularly leaders within an organization, merge their survival with the survival of the organization as a whole, the number of hazards both perceived and actual surge. As a result, the organization's identity shifts based on who is in power the threats they consider and the stories they are living.

Organizations that use the values they purport as the standard to assess themselves tend to conceptualize threats and the potential threats they respond to with slightly different approaches. When values are thought to be the driving agent of organizational action, often members of the community can feel obliged to subscribe to particular points of view consistent with the identified values. Certainly, that approach induces a congruence between policy and practice, but it sometimes has an unintended consequence of restraining important organizational discourse and growth that is often born out of healthy philosophical variance. More importantly, when people feel culturally, intellectually, or socially restrained it is sometimes difficult for them to reach their maximum potential and productivity. Sometimes disagreements are not open and as a result private and passive tensions build up over time that when left unchecked present a range of perils for the organization that can include the survival of the organization itself. Chief among the challenges is the ability of the organization to operate at its optimum efficiency. In some cases, these tensions can encourage practices that work against organizational interests and consequently threatens its existence. Often feeding a potential for destruction from within.

Ontology

Often these combinations of factors have a direct and indirect impact what is understood as the organization's nature of being. While every organization has to constantly confront what it believes is its nature of being, that collective quest becomes significantly more convoluted when leaders in the organization align the organization's survival with their own. In such instances, organizations are in danger of being less driven by their stated mission, goals, and values, more driven by the fears, concerns, and interests of individual decision makers. This often results in what can be referred to as an organizational identity crisis. The nature of an organization's being is less clear to its members and severely impairs its ability to be efficient and productive. Members of the organization tend to align organizational practice with the interests of leaders rather than with organizational values in part because in such circumstances organizational values and goals are effectively replaced by the wants of decision makers. This is often further complicated because to varying degrees the interests of leaders are understood and executed by members.

As a result, some people are more in line with a leader's individual interest and others operate more in line with organization's stated mission, values, and goals when they are different. Members of the organization are knowingly and often unknowingly working across purposes. Some are serving the interests of a particular leader that are stated and interests that are assumed and others are attempting to execute practice supported by the stated and assumed values of the organization. These kinds of dynamics are exactly what is needed to create an organizational identity crisis consequently feeding the elements necessary for its destruction. A collective and shared understanding of an organization's nature of being, its ontology, has a meaningful impact on not only the organization's productivity, but more importantly to its survival. When the understanding is shared resources can be allocated, performances can be evaluated, and outcomes can be assessed in ways that are cogent and in line with the organization's endurance in difficult times.

An organization's ontology is vital to its ability to identify its competitive landscape, serve its purpose and respond to perceived threats and challenges because it provides a realistic understanding of its strengths and weaknesses. A healthy and collective assessment of an organization's ontology helps inform important questions that every organization must answer such as: What kinds of members help drive organizational success? What are our current organizational gaps that challenge our ability to respond to anticipated obstacles? Are there ongoing difficulties we face based on the nature of our being? What strengths does the nature of our being provide us with? What challenges are unique to our environment? Each of these questions and many others improve an organization's ability to assess danger and respond to threats. Most of all a clear understanding of an organization's ontology provides the capacity to defend the space it believes is worthy to inhabit.

Culture

No identity development happens in a vacuum for individuals or organizations, it is always a process that involves multiple components interrelating, networking, and intermingling simultaneously. Where ontology requires an organization to see itself in the mirror, culture refers to the social interactions of the people who make up the organization. Certainly, behavior is always connected to the understanding one has for its nature of being, but they are not necessarily one in the same.

15

Culture is never simply the values an organization may espouse; it is also rooted in the way those values are expressed and interpreted by the people who operate within any organization. Culture frames both acceptable social behavior within an organization and the methods to ensure compliance. Moreover, culture examines the extent to which behavior facilitates productivity and identifies consequences when it is a hindrance.

While organizational culture is often measured by the values implicitly and explicitly condoned by policy and practice, it also has a direct impact on a member's enthusiasm, cooperation, and commitment. Organizations short on any one of those elements or any combination of the three tend to have higher turnover. When people are not satisfied or self-actualized within an organizational structure not only are they less efficient and often less reliable, oftentimes they leave. Organizational culture speaks to the bonds within its community, but more importantly it impacts on the commitment they have to the organization itself. When people leave in noteworthy numbers over time it compromises institutional memory and directly damages efficiency in ways that can be measured by time on task, resources to train new people, and critical operational gaps that are often the result of such departures. Organizational culture informs us of the reasons people leave, the number of people who leave and the impact on operations. It also impacts on an organization's ability to attract new members and their concomitant talents and energy. In the ongoing effort to survive new members expand organizational capacity and by their very presence new members support the organizations effort to endure. Organizational culture reflects not only the values an organization claims, but it also speaks to its willingness or ability to realize the expression of those values in the way people behave with one another inside the organization, the way the organization carries out its mission, and ultimately the way threats and challenges are handled both internally and externally.

Organizational culture at its essence should be a factor that sustains its endurance rather than amplify challenges and risks. It either becomes an adhesive that binds a community together or it is laxative that unties it from its mission and the people who are charged to carry it out. Organizational culture is never impartial or unbiased because it is a driver for strategic planning, performance evaluations, and organizational initiatives. It creates an environment that supports human dignity, or it does not. Certainly, it is possible to change organizational culture, but it is not an easy endeavor because it requires an organizational self-assessment process that must have the intent to reveal all the ways in which the organization falls short in the areas that matter to it. In such processes, values, intent, and outcomes must be explicit so as to provide a way forward that allows everyone to understand both the reason and the need for change.

Organizational culture is no small thing, it is in many ways the mechanism that organizations use to justify their existence, the permissions they extend to defend it and a realization of the sacrifices they are willing to make for their own endurance. No organization is without values and goals that explain its reason for being, to itself and to all others. More than simply its reason for being organizations develop procedures and processes for how it operates and those operations both implicitly and explicitly provide permissions and prohibitions. Organizational culture is a tangible tool that is utilized by its community that guides expectations, training, communication, and a generalized understanding of systemic happenings. As such it is both nuanced and specific consequently it is also transparent and unclear. The role of culture in organizational identity and survival cannot be understated, because very often it is reason for survival or the cause of a demise.

The variance of organizational structures ranges greatly, but what connects them all is the requirement to assess its membership understanding for its reason for being. Moreover, every organization must set itself apart from other similar associations; while appreciating the commonalities they have to others in the same industry. Every organization in some way arranges itself to respond to the needs of its community in one way or another. The notion of family meets these organizational criteria in ways that are obvious and in others that are not.

Family (sociological, traditions, values)

The idea and construction of family is one of the most fundamental versions of human organization. Families of all sorts; culturally, biologically and otherwise require the same elements as any other organization, and every family must respond to similar organizational challenges. A family must constitute its membership, come to terms with its ontology, and grapple with its culture, its impact and its effect on its members' interactions. A family's identity like other organizations is assessed by examining its stated mission, goals, and vision against its practices. A family must understand the space it occupies, what that space means to its members, and determine how they defend themselves against threats individually as well as collectively. While many understand family as biological constructions, their sociological worthiness extends well beyond any simplistic biological connections one might identify.

Families like all organizations are burdened with the obligation to survive and they are required to assess their strengths and vulnerabilities in that effort. The effort of families to assess themselves is in part an aspect of their identity. Familial identity is informed by not only the emotional and biological connections that serve as its basis, but notions of family are simultaneously informed by our sense of self while being confronted by various individual growth patterns, psychological shifts, and emotional needs. Familial identity tends to imprint each of its members with common values, experiences and events, but the understanding and meaning of those elements can and does vary as each member seeks to construct the story they serve as their individual and collective identity. The impact of family on individual identity development is critical because the resulting story that becomes an individual identity is constantly responding to questions about reality that often have their origins in one's earliest understandings of familial operations and dynamics.

Families are required to respond to incredibly complex circumstances while also having to make very specific choices. Families like other organizations identify behaviors that are prohibited and permitted, and those specific choices have a significant impact on their member development and perception. While families without question make countless numbers of specific choices that contribute to their members' stories, they also respond to broad societal happenings. The notion of family informs understandings of broad concepts such as love, acceptance, forgiveness, truth, other, loyalty, and almost any other meaningful concept held by most people. The importance of family is grounded in the development of its members in both the things the family formally addresses and in the things that it does not. The sociological importance of family, the values they advance and the traditions they use to solidify their space in the world are in some ways different from other organizational structures and in other ways they are similar. Nonetheless the perception of our survival and the threats perceived as a unit and individually are inextricably linked to the understanding and meaning that each of us has for our family history.

Sociological

A sociological perspective of family or any other organization is instrumental in understanding not just the roles they play and their daily operation; a sociological understanding highlights the societal factors to which families, and any other organization must respond. Moreover, it helps identify the social factors that create the need for family as well as the role family plays in identity development. Family is the first social structure to provide information that helps to both explain the world we perceive and our understanding of our place in it. Even in the absence of family, each of us is compelled to gather data that furthers our survival, of course physically, but also in other ways we determine to be important and relevant. Either with the support of family and even in its absence, very early in our development we begin to connect the information we collect with our understanding of our perceived reality.

Sociologically the covenant of family provides shelter, food and support necessary for survival. However, more broadly familial operations establish the foundation upon which we build the skills necessary to negotiate and navigate our individual identity development and the perception of survival that results. Early in our development we are bound to answer questions such as; who am I and to whom do I belong? Once families or early caregivers inculcate responses to those questions into the early development of its members, the implications tend to have a significant and lasting impact on the stories we tell ourselves for both our identity development and the threats we perceive to our survival.

Very early in our journey to understand our place in the world we encounter deeply ceded fears and expectations that serve as the framework for the world we perceive. Undoubtedly those early perceptions are either nurtured or curbed by the developmental process and what is inculcated by the family and/or caregivers. In the very beginning of one's ability to perceive the world around them, there is often a compulsion to inquire about why things are the way they are. Not simply for a general curiosity, however that is certainly a factor, we are confronted with an innate obligation to seek understanding of the world to construct our place in it. The role of family or the lack thereof in this process imprints not just answers to posed questions but also a generalized orientation to challenges, problem solving, and self-regulation.

The question of identity development is not simply shaped by the early operations of family dynamics; it is affirmed or repudiated continuously in the lifelong journey to get to know ourselves. Certainly, family is not the only information source that informs the story we tell ourselves to explain our place in the world we perceive.

As the developmental process proceeds the dominance of family as an information source is challenged by a host of other sources but whatever has been imprinted early in the developmental process is never all together replaced. However, family dynamics are not simply responding to the societal dynamics they are simultaneously informed by them. Consequently, while families are preparing their members for the world outside them, they are also being impacted by the changes and circumstances they face. To such an extent that the very notion of what and who constitutes family can be modified in a given individual life and/or in a given cultural community. These potentially constant shifts in family dynamics make it difficult to analyze with any precision to determine the exact impact family has on the identity developmental process except to say the role of family is irreplaceable on the journey to understand ourselves.

Traditions and values

In an ever-changing world where information flow is widespread, inconsistent, contradictory, weaponized and deliberately distorted, families of all sorts face an almost insurmountable task of centering themselves on a set of traditions and values that affirm the truths upon which they believe they are based. As such, families are required to develop activities that they believe strengthen and reaffirm their bonds, encourage the growth of their members, and enhance their members' ability to navigate social, emotional, spiritual and of course physical hazards that are anticipated and those that are not. Families avoid this responsibility at their own risk on several fronts. The process to explain our place in the world is unending and so too is the identity development process. When families are absent in the ever-present need that each of us must seek the meaning of our place in the world, we leave our members vulnerable to information sources whose intents are often less clear and most often not born of any need to strengthen familial bonds.

Amid the chaos and confusion, we call life, each family is obligated to discover and execute activities that remind us of lessons taught, affirm our value, and enhance our ability to navigate the unknown. While every member of the family will uniquely approach these arenas in ways that are distinctive to their own understanding of what the life they live means to them, family activities are events that are singularly centered in their ability to feed one's spirit. Family activities encourage us to see possibilities in our story, or they remind us of hazards and insecurities that heighten our perception of the potential threats. It is not uncommon for one to feel familial endeavors as some combination of the two, but nonetheless important to us.

Family traditions are activities in which members engage both separately and collectively. Moreover, traditions are the activities that express the values that help explain a family's place in the world. The values represented in traditions are the foundation of how a family sees itself and the world to which it is responding. All the while informing an often implicit and persistent compulsion to gain insight into: what brings us Joy? What reveals our fears? How do we measure "our better?" To what extent are we whole and healthy? And how do we concern ourselves with that part of us that needs nourishment? The traditions and values of a family provide its members with information reservoirs that are utilized on the journey "to know thy self." In the best version of family dynamics each member is encouraged to share space with the perceived best version of themselves. However, when there is a gap between the perceived best version of oneself and one's most authentic self, that gap is often filled with fear and insecurity. When the gap exists it must also be accounted for in the journey to understand our value, the bigger the gap the more explanation that is required.

There should be no doubt that family is a crucial element in the journey to understand our place in the world and the stories we tell ourselves to justify our worth. While family events are shared experiences our understanding of them is not, each member tells themselves a story that explains their perception and justifies their place both within and outside the family. Family traditions and values are indispensable in the effort to authentically understand the identity development process, but it is even more crucial to understand what those events and values mean to its members. No family operates in a vacuum; they are the foundation of any society or civilization. The impact of family on the individual identity development process is both complex and important, however the society that surrounds and encloses the family is also extremely significant in a process that is uneven, steadfast, and comprehensive.

National Identity Development

National identity development is a construct that informs international relations to include war and economics. At the same time national identity informs the construction of family, the educational process of children, and the expectations, dreams and fears for the entire population of a given nation/country. In that way national identity development may be the single biggest contributor to human activity and cultural production. It may be the largest and most far-reaching organization on the planet. Far reaching in the sense that there is almost no human perception, idea or activity that is not shaped by the national context that produces it. While the impact of national identity is undeniable in a host of human endeavors to certainly include the process of identity development, however it is not an easy thing to define, explain, and distinguish as a phenomenon unto itself.

The modern nation/state system is not without challenges in the area of identity development. While there are nations whose national identities were forged over hundreds and sometimes thousands of years like France, England, Ghana, Mexico, Sweden, Denmark, Germany and China just to name a few; however, there are hundreds of countries whose identity development process was interrupted by cultural hegemony, political and economic exploitation, not to mention the exacerbation of natural human conflict for the purposes of imperialism and domination. As such, it would include most of the nations on the continent of Africa and South America, many of the countries on the Asian continent to include the "middle east" and certainly the vast majority of the countries in Central America. No serious examination of national identity development for most nations around the world would leave the impact of these factors unaddressed. However, those are better factors left to historical analyses specific to each nation, in part because every nation is unique in one way or another. However, a piece like this is not well suited to provide an in-depth analysis of each nation/state in the world, nonetheless national identity development is too important a concept leave unaddressed.

It does not matter about the circumstance under which a country came into being or even its current circumstance, as with all organizations a country must define its space, justify its worthiness to exist to itself and to others, and lastly it must defend itself against all perceived threats both internal and external. National identities are not only composed of shared values, ideas, world views and interests of a given population. Too often the shared delusions, fears, and anxieties of a given population inform their collective identity in ways that are often difficult to measure with any precision but too important to ignore. With no exceptions every country has people who are more privileged and disadvantaged than others, the gap in the inequality ranges based on different measurements. In the case of national identity, it is more important to understand the mental models employed that encourage the disadvantaged to see their interests aligned with those in power. National history is replete with examples of people in disadvantaged circumstances whose identities so diverge from those in power that they separate to form new national identities, and subsequently new nations.

Nations like any other organization must present its members with the promise of realizing realities together that are otherwise unachievable. In this effort nations create institutions that provide members/citizens with services and products that they (members/citizens) can't create for themselves. These institutions in theory are designed to support its members/citizens in their pursuit of shared dreams, goals and values. The operation of these institutions is designed to rise above identities not shared by the entire population that may include things like race, sex, ethnicity, religion, sexual orientation or any other sense of self that could compete with a national identity. National identity is subject to all the factors of any other organizational identity. Nations as a collective must confront their ontology, the nature of their existence. A nation's ontology is rarely uncontested among its citizens; the strength and depth of the contest is rooted in the extent to which people see national institutions operating in their interests or the interests of the collective.

National identity development is true to form is understood from the inside out, to fully understand national identity it must be understood from the vantage point of its population. National identity in one form or another forces a collective answer to questions like; what does it means to "be." As with all forms of identity development individual or otherwise; nations like individuals are compelled to defend the space they occupy physically as well as psychologically. The survival of a nation is directly related to its ability to define the space it occupies, but it is simultaneously subject to its ability to forge a collective identity development process shared by its citizenry. As with other organizations, nations are evaluated not only by their shared values, ideas and aspirations but also by the permissions it gives itself to achieve those goals. When leaders of a given nation substitute their individual interests for collective will the potential for national demise is born.

The nature of a nation is evidenced both in its espoused beliefs and principles but expressed in its policy, law and practices. As with any other organization, the extent to which a nation's espoused beliefs are in conflict with its policy, law, and practice is the extent to which there is an identity crisis. In such cases, citizens of a country or members of an organization are often divided between those who see leaders as the expression of the collective and those who perceive a gap in the stated values, goals, and behaviors of the nation and the actions and direction of those charged with responsibility to make decisions. When any nation's identity development process is confronted with an identity crisis it often results in conflict that threatens possibility of collective aspiration. The depth of the conflict is informed by the extent to which citizens perceive the threat to be in opposition to the nation's nature of being, its ontology.

Nations whose identity development process has been forged over many hundreds of years if not thousands have a distinct advantage over nations whose identity development process has been interrupted by sustained colonialism, cultural hegemony, political and economic exploitation and any other factors that have damaged a nation's ability to develop a collective sense of self. While certainly every nation is confronted with the continuous challenge to hold together the collective during difficult times, each national history uniquely positions a particular country in its resources and methods to do so. The history of a nation informs its cultural framework to resolve such conflicts. In such cases nations are regularly challenged by the cultural permissions granted to decision makers to respond to actual and perceived threats to a collective identity. How much pain, force and coercion are acceptable to install an understanding to a shared awareness of what it means to "be?" Is the realization of a shared sense of what it means to "be" guided by prescribed principles and beliefs or more motivated by the accumulation of power and the expression of it? National identity development processes are required to explain to the whole what the collective means. To some the process by which that shared sense of identity is determined is as important as the outcome, but to others realizing and imposing that identification becomes its own justification.

Nations like other organizations must assess the behavioral cultural permissions they give themselves to realize their goals. Nations and organizations who are required to adhere to certain beliefs and principles seek the meaning of their identity to a fidelity of an established standard. However, there are others whose identity is rooted in the power to impose a collective vision and in such cases the results take precedence over the processes. In nations where fidelity to the standard is a chief factor in the identity development process; the threats to the process are often perceived as existential. However, in nations where the result is important the threats to the power to impose the collective vision are often viewed as existential. The cultural restraints on policy and practice in nations where the process itself is an important aspect of identity are significantly different from nations where the power to impose is restrained only by its ability to realize the result.

As nations engage in the continuous process of identity development and grapple with questions that speak to the nature of their existence. They are both informed by and assessed by the cultural permissions they give themselves to realize and forge a collective sense of self. The cultural permission to engage in policy and practice designed to develop a shared sense of self are not only connected to how those policies and practices realize their espoused ideals, but they measure the extent to which they are willing to ensure that citizens are justly impacted by the outcomes. When citizens are knowingly over time unfairly obstructed from realizing shared dreams and goals the disparities that result is factored into the identify development process; both the result of the policies and categories of people who are jammed by the effects.

When a national identity development process is confronted with a crisis that is born out of a competition between what is promised and practices to fulfill the promise, like any other organization they are less able to defend the space they believe they are worthy of occupying. In those circumstances they are less able to appropriately assess external threats, violating a fundamental element of survival. For something to live it must defend the space it believes makes it worthy of survival. A nation identity development process represents its most efficient defense mechanism because it is the basis to conceptualize threats, determine responses and provide the cultural permissions necessary to ensure its survival. When a national identity development process is in crisis, its ability to do any of those things effectively and efficiently is diminished significantly. It is in danger of being a nation confronted with an existential threat that it is unprepared to address.

When a nation's identity development process is confronted with a significant identity crisis its resolution is often rooted in an emphasis on a shared vision born out communal values, ideas and goals or pooled together by fears, failures and delusions. Each can and does result in different cultural permissions and understandings. When collectives draw upon common values, ideas and goals they are invited to share in a public process that lights their path forward. However, when they are encouraged to delve into common fears, failures and delusions there tends to be less emphasis on lighting a common path as it is a desire to darken the path of others. When emphasis is placed on the shared fears, failures and delusions it often gives permission to impose the necessary harm and pain to bring about a collective malnourished vision that is rooted in turmoil. Such a vision is sustainable, but it requires the turmoil to maintain its collective image. When an emphasis for collective identity development is placed on shared values, goals, and ideas; sustainability is rooted in an effort to realize the best version of a collective self rather than a need for a villain or villains as the case may be.

National identities, however, are not often one or the other they often draw from elements of both. Indeed, national identity development often has within it all the elements necessary to damage and/or destroy it; all that is necessary is to nourish those aspects of national identity that relate to fears rather than shared values. When a collective identity is fueled by an aggression or animosity of an "other" its survival is determined by the extent to which a united identity can be sustained by targeting that "other" rather than fostering a collective path forward to realize a healthy cooperative identity.

III.

THE ROLE OF OTHERNESS IN IDENTITY DEVELOPMENT

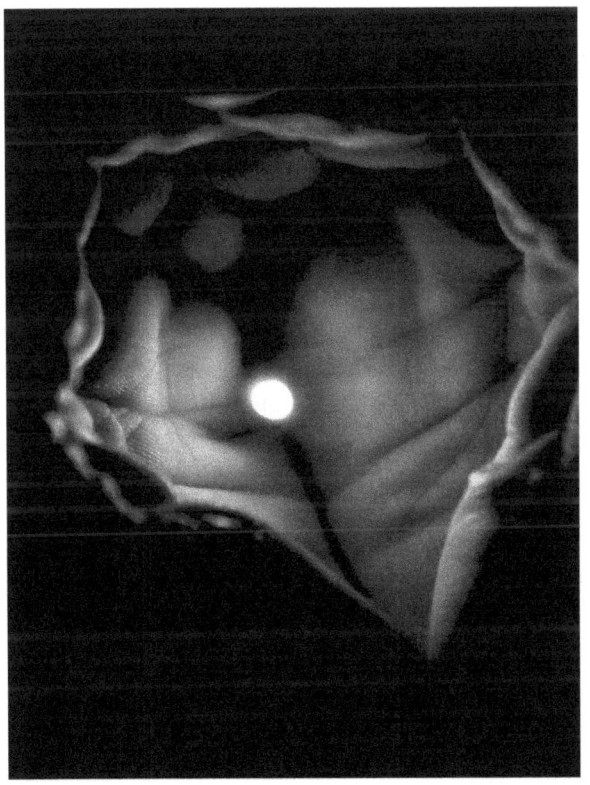

Otherness explored

The concept of an "other" is not new, it is an idea that many scholars have explored in a variety of arenas (literary, religious, sociological, and otherwise) to include identity development. The importance of an "other" is rooted in the human need to explain the unknown in each of our anecdotes. In any given lived experience, there is much more that is unknown than there is known. As a result, while we seek to construct, understand and explain the stories that provide meaning for our worthiness, we are simultaneously unconsciously cognizant that our accounts are often incomplete. While the acknowledgement of the inadequacy of our stories is often unconscious, the creation of an "other" serves a psychological space filler to color-in blank spots. The manufacturing of an "other" in some ways is an indispensable part of the identity development process.

The production of an "other" allows the identity development process to continue when important data is insufficient, absent, or even contradictory. Each of those categories describes a considerable quantity of the space we are required to navigate on the trek to realize our significance. Without the presence of an "other" oftentimes we would be forced into stagnation when movement is required, needed or sought. The formation of an "other" is in part why the process to get to know ourselves is unending, it provides the mechanism to move on when we encounter elements that threaten our psychological well-being or occupy an unidentified arena of our existence. The "other" is a tool to deal with unsolved versions of difference that threaten the realities to which we wish to respond. In short, an "other" is often a part of our sense of self that requires growth skills that we have yet to develop.

Who are we not?

The journey to understanding our place in the world is informed by what we think we know and believe, and it is also informed by our perception of the unknown. On the occasions that we are confronted with uncertainty, doubt, newness and even strange aspects of the world we understand and our place in it; we are still required to locate and value ourselves. There is a tendency to see circumstances that are unspecified as hazardous, in part because it is difficult to determine what is secure or even benign when things appear vague and unreliable. As such when we are in physical, psychological, and/or social surroundings that don't comport to anything to which we are familiar, we are then left to our values, beliefs, fears, hopes and dreams to locate ourselves and our perceived survival.

Because more of the world is unknown to us than it is known we spend as much time as possible in the spaces that give credence to the stories, we are telling ourselves about who we are, why we are and what we believe we are, other realities are often beyond are conscious experience. Since survival is often predicated on the ability to predict and understand one's environment, it stands to reason that the absence of predictability and understanding tends to be viewed as an actual or potential threat. As we roam the terrain, we call our lives we generally confine ourselves to the familiar because we believe we understand the dangers and safe places. The stories we tell ourselves about who we are can be affirmed in ways that are comforting, and we learn to live with circumstances that trouble our stories by being mildly aware of their existence but never spending much time in the spaces we believe leave us vulnerable.

Any notion or understanding of survival is reasonably vulnerable in spaces that are undefined and tentative. Under such circumstances it would make sense to connect survival to the familiar and danger to that which is unknown, uncertain, unpredictable, or sometimes that includes things that are new. If one is not careful it is possible to connect the concept of change itself to danger because it is often accompanied by many of the factors that challenge survival. The constant presence and impact of change can make the familiar, unfamiliar. If identity development is the result of the story or stories that we tell ourselves to explain both why we exist and why that existence is worthy of the space it occupies, change requires those stories to be constantly updated, adjusted, modified, affirmed and ultimately evaluated in their usefulness in aiding our endurance.

If change is constant, it requires an unending effort to construct stories that enhance our understanding of who we are based on factors

31

we observe and absorb, for people who are not willing or capable of doing the work it makes more sense to understand who you are not. Determining who you are not creates a space perfectly suited psychologically, socially, and even spiritually to house the "other." The construction of an "other" provides a convenient catch all to explain all the uncertainties that are an inevitable part of living that is filled with blind turns, dark tunnels and uncomfortable truths. When confronted with uncertainty, doubt and even originality it is decidedly easier to explain who you aren't than it is to do the work that reveals who you are to yourself. Whatever you believe you are not simply becomes a characteristic assigned to the "other" (the other race, woman, religion, community, nation, family, organization or whatever else we encounter that we don't want to deal with).

The construction of the "other" serves no other purpose than to provide a comfortable mechanism to not do the work necessary to understand your true self. It's simply a constructed identity that is in no way based on any external data except that which we create in our imaginations. The "other" provides us with to permission to move on when we encounter a circumstance that we either cannot understand, or we choose not to. In either case we can simply move on because we superficially determine it is not compatible with the story that explains who we are to ourselves, but we often are not required to examine why, nor are we compelled to identify any similarities we may share. The "other" in many ways reflects that part of our story we wish to leave untold, as a result it becomes who we are not.

Who do we not want to be?

The construction of the "other" is not simply bound by a desire to avoid that part of reality that does not affirm our stories, it also provides a target for the expression of vaguely conceived frustrations that often accompany the willful ignorance connected to denying complicated parts of ourselves. While "who we are not" is a more settled sense of denial individuals, organizations and even nations have often located and identified the areas to be avoided and as such we fabricate individual and collective delusions to help navigate around the spaces determined to be dangerous. However, who we do not want to be is a less settled denial because in this notion of the "other" there are undeniable similarities or at least connections that do not allow for its complete dismissal. Who we do not want to be is born out of a psychological and often social need to not be confused with something we don't like, don't value, or generally resent.

Where the "other" in the who we are not denial tends to be conceived in a manner that is absolute (of course until it is not), the "other" that is fueled by the denial of who we don't want to be is often familiar and as such is less dismissible in an absolute sense. Who we don't want to be is energized simultaneously by our apparent genuine revulsion and our often-unconscious connection to it. This "other" presents a special kind of danger to our perception because its existence risks an exposure of a vulnerability or vulnerabilities that warrants in our estimation the risk of death itself. An "other" that is framed out of a desperation to keep unrevealed those aspects of our identity that to our judgement are completely defenseless pose the most significant threat to ourselves and those we assess as the "other."

Where we learn to develop an irrational equilibrium with the "other" that is imagined out of our absolute delusion about who we are not, there is a tendency to lack the wiliness to do so with "other" that is conceived out of who we don't want to be. Its presence is a constant reminder of psychological, spiritual, and other kinds of susceptibilities that produce a version of fear that is unresolvable and incompatible with the stories we use to explain our existence. As a result, the conflict with the "other" imagined out of who we don't want to be is always at violent risk because it is easy to conclude that the existence of one is predicated on the destruction of the "Other."

The construction of the "other" in the identity development process is impossible to avoid because it provides the ability to fill holes in our reality that we have no other way of satiating. Consequently, it is important to understand that any attempt for us to grapple with the construction of the "other" has to be rooted in the role it plays in our perception of our own worth most importantly to ourselves. Our desire to tell ourselves stories that explain our value, strengths, weaknesses, purpose, and whatever else is necessary to defend the space we occupy is not an option. The stories we tell are necessary to ensure our endurance during trying times. Moreover, it is impossible to live without the presence of unknowns, uncertainties, uncomfortable truths, and fears. The existence of the "other" provides us with a tool to understand the ugly and uneasy parts of our identities. The "other" is in part an attempt to deal with the fears that are generated out of our limited perceptions and abilities. When our fears are not constrained by our hopes, dreams and values, or even worse subjugates them, the "other" becomes a convention to makes ourselves feel better about all the things we wish were but are not. The presence of fear cannot be separated from the construction of the "other" and as such it requires special attention.

The role of fear

Fear plays an interesting and complex role in the desire to survive and endure events and happenings that potentially injure, damage, or challenge the stories we use to explain our worth. One reason for this complexity is fear often serves as an important asset in the effort to withstand encounters perceived as alarming. Survival in any duration requires a healthy perception and understanding of any potentially perilous effects. Fear as an asset invites caution often exactly when it is necessary, moreover fear generally provokes and encourages the actions necessary to overcome a perceived test.

Fear, however, is not an on/off switch in an absolute sense, it is more like a light dimmer, certainly there are times when the light is dim and there are other times when the light is bright but then there is everything in between. Fear, when it is dim, is comparable to the hairs standing up on the back of someone's neck, a knot in the stomach or a distinguishable concern without a clear and rational reason for it. When the light is bright of course one is often presented with the extreme classic fight or flight scenario. However, fear is a factor in the development process far more often than when we are forced into making extreme decisions.

Concern and caution belong to the family of perspectives that fear governs, often in ways that are healthy and rational. They motivate one to construct action paths that try to account for understood hazards and evaluate reasonable risks. In the process of identity development these concerns don't generally threaten our stories, in fact more often than not they justify them. Concerns and cautions provide affirmation for our stories in ways that are demonstrable both in the world outside our control and in the one we imagine in our minds. Concern and caution are often allies in both the desire and the effort to protect ourselves in any way we determine to be important, spiritually, emotionally, psychologically and ultimately physically. The desire to survive is the chief reason for the existence of fear, while it is sometimes thought of as a barrier it could be better understood as a protector, even though it is both and more.

When the light is dim it gives one the option to adjust our stories subtly and sometimes even unconsciously. It provides a safe environment for our stories to undergo modification on terms that maintain our comfort and confirm our stories in the ways that are most important to us. But it is imperative that it be understood that the comfort our fears provide in the form of concerns and caution is not safety, it is merely seeing the world and our place in it in a way that matches a story we are making up in our imagination. There is no doubt that the stories are informed by information we gather from our environment, but it is our story that connects the pieces of data in ways that are unique to our perception, and they make us safer only to the extent that our perceptions and the happenings around us match. For most of us that is the case far less often than we would like to admit, but it is comfortable and sometimes comfort is confused with safety. Moreover, sometimes unconsciously we accept comfort because real safety requires attentiveness and alertness that for most of us is mentally and physically exhausting.

The role fear plays in the construction of the "other" as a factor in the identity development process can never be overstated. In its extreme it can fuel irrational responses to exposures that are verifiable and those that are not, in its more subtle forms it often softly coerces action paths that affirm familiar comforts of over uncertain growth. None among us is above the choice, while certainly there is variance in the decisions, we make based on the stories we are living. The construction of the "other" is an important dynamic both in the assessing our value and identifying the threats that endanger our perceived place in the world. Our fears often produce the need for the "other" and they provide with the necessary impetus to guard against them.

Resolution of fear in an absolute sense is not an option on the menu, however an effort to understand some of the motivations that give the fears we perceive the power to impact our activities, decisions, assessments, and ultimately our stories is always possible. While fear provides an environment that is fertile with the components necessary to construct the "other," it also provides a useful awareness of actual dangers. Sometimes fear alerts us to dangers that require our response, while also contributing to a calculation that overplays the potential risk. Fear will always have the potential to do great damage both real and imagined because of its role as a protector. However, when we account for what is being protected and why, we can provide the protector with the comfort necessary to envision and discern a version of safety that fulfills its obligation and the tools necessary to overcome any potential barriers that result from fear. When fear is outlined by the energy of hope and aspiration its ability to gauge potential risk is enhanced significantly because it is forced to balance apparent threats with potential rewards.

The role hope and aspiration

The steady confrontation with the unknown and its relationship with the construction of the "other" has a variance in both its outcomes and its inputs. Fear's impact on the inputs and outcomes is undeniable; however, the role of hope and aspiration is no less significant or complex. Where fear places an emphasis on the dynamics that tend to suggest warnings, aspiration with hope tends to accent factors that can enhance, improve, and enrich the stories we believe explain our sense of being. Where fear naturally averts the unknown hope with aspiration connects notions of possibility and growth to the spaces that actually and potentially challenge the stories we want to live. When fear is balanced with hope and aspiration the stories we tell can have a different orientation with uncertainty and the unknown.

Uncertainty is a natural predator of comfort and safety as well as it should be, there should always be at least a healthy awareness of things we don't understand and things with which we have limited experiences. Hope with aspiration is not a panacea in the ever-present bout with fear. While hope and aspiration are important elements of growth and learning, they are not particularly well suited to serve as protectors. While they tend to invite an awareness to possibilities that both enhance and enrich our identities, they can sometimes underestimate a potential risk. However, hope with aspiration adds more sophistication to the lens in which we see ourselves and the world around us; providing more depth to the perspectives we have about the world and our place in it.

The impact of hope and aspiration on our identity development process is critical. While hope is centered in anticipation of the light even when it is dark, aspiration tends to be rooted in the opportunities we imagine the light offers. As we seek to explain our worth to ourselves and others, with the added complexity of devising stories that inform the meaning of the spaces we occupy. The journey we call our lives is inevitably impacted by both our fears, our hopes and our aspirations. There is no clear metric to determine how much of either is used in any individual's identity development or sense of self, except to say it is

37

probably observable in particular moments when one is more motivated by one or the other. However, every moment that follows provides new spaces and opportunities that are not obligated to conform to historical patterns, but they often do exactly that. The construction of an "other" in the identity development process is crucial to both responding and relating to that part of our existence that is unknown and uncertain. Each of us is required to develop patterns or systemically relate to our uncertainty because of its ubiquitous presence in our reality. If we don't have patterns to guide us in moments of uncertainty, doubt, and confrontation, we would be forced to constantly arrange responses to the extent that there would be little time to do much else. The "other" which can also be understood as a personalized unknown would render our ability to operate in uncontrolled realities nearly useless.

Relating with the unknown

Relating to the unknown is quite possibly the single most underrated aspect of the identity development process. The art of telling ourselves stories that explain our meaning in a world that is in many ways beyond our comprehension is an effort that is irrational by its very nature. The ongoing battle between the unknown and the effort to contend with it fuels both the identity development process and the stories we construct to explain our trek through it. Both the starting point and the destination are matters of significant contention with little possibility of distinct resolution. Nonetheless each of us in our own way moves to bring as much understanding to our journey as we can, not because we are certain that the answers are within our grasp, because our movement and storytelling often only confirm our limitations, vulnerabilities, and deepest fears that knowing was and likely will never be an option. Consequently, the role of fear and aspiration are required to help us relate to that which we may never understand.

Relating to the unknown is fundamental to the effort to explain our worth to ourselves. Our identity development process forces us to confront both our fears and our hopes about what we believe this life has to offer. When our relationship with the unknown is guided by hope and aspiration, we are more likely to see possibilities and opportunities to grow in times of uncertainty, but when our relationship with the unknown is informed by our fears we are more likely to concern ourselves with those things that challenge our growth and decrease our ability to learn and adapt. Some may suggest the difference is a matter of choice but to do so is a considerable over-simplification. There is no question that there are elements of choice involved in any and every decision, but it must always be understood that the identity development process is much more complex than a series of choices and/or decisions. In our confrontations with the unknown, uncertainty, challenge and doubt the stories we tell ourselves can become revelations that tend to uncover what drives our movement. Rarely are the actions we take in those moments born out of conscious awareness; however, they do reveal motivational elements of our sense of self that tend to be fed by hope and aspiration or fear. In such cases each of us gains more insight into ourselves and if we are wise stewards with the information our sense of being is enhanced by both the process and the experience.

Our relationship with the unknown informs both our motivation and our connection to the construction of an "other." While the source of an "other" tends to be the imagination it is constantly confronted by the world outside us and consequently, we are forced to assimilate information that both confirms and contradicts its existence. Our relationship with the unknown is closely related to the construction of the "other" in that they are both related to the effort to process things, people, actions and events that escape our comprehension. Comprehension, understanding, and predictability are often essential elements to our perceived endurance and developing patterns that make it so. The stories we tell ourselves to explain our worth in moments of uncertainty, doubt and challenge feed our sense of meaning in terms of our fears or aspirations but frequently both simultaneously. How we perceive our survival is intimately connected to the way we contend with the ever-present presence of the unknown.

IV.

SURVIVAL: THE ESSENCE OF IDENTITY DEVELOPMENT

Survival concept or reality

S urvival is an interesting if not complicated concept when its pursuit results in 100% failure. Ultimately all life in one way or another ends sooner or later, most things that have a beginning have an end. If the end is inevitable, what does survival mean? Is survival a psychological adaptation of something more akin to endurance? To be sure, the answers to questions like these are deeply rooted in the understanding one has about their sense of self. The impact of spiritual and other non-temporal concepts of being are relevant to many people and their understanding of such ideas makes the physical presence much less relevant to the idea of survival. While it is an incontrovertible fact that all living things will eventually not be living things, does that indeed mean that they are no longer surviving.

Does a record, a memory, a video, or any other mechanism that preserves the essence of one's existence constitute survival? There is no doubt that the answer to such existential crises can vary significantly given the story or stories one is living. Identity development is informed not just by the stories we tell ourselves but also by what we think those stories mean in a broader understanding of existence. To many people the understanding of survival is not limited to physical parameters, those notions of survival tend to be more fluid and freeing; couched in concepts of energy, belief, feeling and understanding. Identity development is an outcome of survival while at the same time being a primary producer of the concept. Identity development is a process that one has to be alive to do, however one's understanding of what constitutes survival is often born out of one's concept of their own sense of reality. The complexities of identity development are never ending, but nonetheless each of is required to continue the effort for as long as we are housed the bodies that we inhabit.

The question of whether survival is a concept or reality is in no way simplistic or unsophisticated, however it is incredibly subjective. Subjective in the sense that each of us is deciding for ourselves with both rational and irrational means and methods. The essence of the question concept or reality allows for the one to account for either, neither or both perspectives on grounds that we determine for ourselves. We do so with absolutely no obligation to justify, explain or defend our perspective to anyone else. We are simply required to ensure for ourselves that our decisions are congruent with the stories we tell ourselves about the meaning of our being. In fact, survival, a concept or reality can compel each of us to access in our imagination not simply for the meaning of our own existence but the meaning of everyone else's existence as well. Providing an opportunity to gain a more intrinsic insight into what we believe may be our own individual ontology. Ultimately it is not something we can be told or gain from any form of analysis; it is something we are required to understand from the inside out.

From the inside out

The process of identity development and even the notion of survival are both phenomena that are deeply personal and private but at the same time they operate in public spaces and impact on everything with which we come in contact. As a result, their impact on the stories we are living is quite profound and meaningful. From the inside out refers to the idea that each of us must investigate our identity development process from inside our own minds, hearts and imaginations. To authentically explore our sense of self, we must give the effort necessary and come to terms with the hopes and fears that drive each of us to act in ways that we believe serve our interest in survival. This effort requires bravery that allows us to look in the darkest places of our identity not because of its evil nature, although for some that might be true, but for most it is necessary to understand how our pains, scars, and concerns have enslaved us to smaller versions of ourselves.

When we strive to share space with better versions of ourselves, we often have to confront and conquer those aspects of us that have not served our interest. Survival is, at its essence, the effort to exist. When we probe our understanding of our worth from the inside out, we must discern the things that we need to feed our soul from the things that bring us pleasure but not joy. What distinguishes them is the impact something has on how you feel about yourself. It is not possible to access that information or awareness from any place other than from the inside out. As such, one must evaluate the consequence something has on the worth they assign to themselves. We are required to notice what we do that compromises the worth we have for ourselves. As we seek to understand the meaning of our existence, it is important that we don't rig the outcome by populating the process with data that lessens the value you have for yourself.

The evaluation process we have for ourselves is persistent and unforgiving, because wherever we go, there we are. In other words, we always deep down inside have a sense of what we believe about our importance and the assets we possess. There is a considerable difference between explaining to yourself why your value is not low and doing the work necessary to demonstrate your significance to the person in the mirror. While from the inside out it will always be grounded in each of our own criteria, it will also have to stand up to the scrutiny of the world around us. What we feel about the inside out will also be sifted through by everyone with which we share space; revealing the confidence that we use to deal with our fears, our understanding of what survival means and how our behavior threatens or supports the existence we conceptualize in our imaginations.

Fear, confidence or understanding

The identity development process is replete with ideas and concepts that have a direct impact on a lived life; to include ideas like worth, comfort, beauty, peace, intuition, threat, safety, and many others. Fundamentally we tend be piloted by the desire to live out our version of our best life or advised by the concerns of all the things that challenge our version of survival. It is difficult to calculate with any precision how any of us feel about why we exist. Moreover, the fears and understandings we have about the world we conceptualize are in many ways uniquely constructed out of the world that each of us calls our reality. The identity development process shifts, adapts, modifies, and reorients, given a varied and variety of inputs it receives from our fears, confidences and understandings.

Our fears are important because they keep us in contact with our limitations, while examining possibilities from the perspective of risk. Many of the most valuable rewards we seek are often connected to hazards that require us to assess our ability to navigate them. The essence of survival is to be aware of any perilous situation and determine the potential damage it can cause. Fear is the mechanism we often use to measure potential losses and as a result its importance is beyond measure. However, fear allows us to prepare potential responses to outcomes that are not welcomed but are predictable. When we are forced to face an unwelcome reality with preparation our confidence to see it through often becomes exactly what it needs to align us with the stories we are living. When we are forced to face things that are unpredictable and unwelcome our understanding of our worth and essence can be challenged in ways that can completely alter who we think we are, good or bad.

It appears that many of who we are physically, psychologically, emotionally, and even spiritually are designed expressly for our survival in the way we understand. Ultimately our confidences, fears, and understandings are rooted in the stories we are living and how we evaluate our worth in them. Our ability to endure the challenges that this life offers is intimately related to what we think about ourselves. However, those perceptions while persistent and durable are not fixed. Our sense of self is often tested against the happenings in the world, and our stories are altered by our capacity to respond to what we encounter. There are none among us whose capacity has not been altered by the turns this life can take, but the outcome is never fixed. If we continue to learn, grow, self-actualize and demonstrate the effort necessary for us to continue, we build on our capacity and ability to see better versions of the people we see in the mirror. Every time we respond to things that challenge the stories we live, and we are forced to grow and learn we develop personal, familial, and even organizational legacies and possibilities that serve our interests and eventually our survival.

Legacy and possibility

Notions of survival are not universal; people understand the concept in a wide range of ways and it's difficult to evaluate one notion as right and another as wrong. In large measures because of the uniqueness of each of our experiences, but sooner or later each of has to confront the fact that our physical bodies will not be here on this earth. Consequently, each of us often feels compelled to determine what that means to us. There is a significant portion of the human population who leave this world without fully fleshing out any rational understanding or strategy. Sometimes they do so because they refuse to address what can be a completely distressing and paralyzing reality and so for their own psychological well-being, they leave the task unmanaged. Of course, there are those who believe they had more time and never got around to the task of examining the state of their current legacy, what that legacy could be and what the possibilities are for the legacies they could leave behind. It may be one of the most unenviable things that humans are destined to do, we are often forced to do it for a loved one or for ourselves and frequently both.

Legacy is not simply how one is remembered but certainly that is an important component of it. Legacy in part speaks to the contributions one either made or makes to the lives of the people that matter to us. It also includes any purpose we use to pilot the happenings of our lives. While certainly there is a clearly selfish element to any concept of survival, our legacies invariably express how we operated and impacted the world we perceive and/or perceived. A legacy answers questions about the impact of our daily decisions and actions to achieve the things we think and think to be important. Our accomplishment of goals, our impact on the lives of others, and the lessons we learned and taught are all important ingredients. Legacies are not formed simply by what we accomplish or impacts one has or had, they are in part informed by how we are; do we live with and on purpose? How did or do we respond to the serious challenges that life often offers? Were and/or are we ambitious in our appetites to do and be better? There are no recipes that serve as a blueprint for legacy development, and it is even possible that people may assign motives to a legacy that did not exist. In that way each of us is at the mercy of the interpreter, those who seek meaning from our journey. All that any one of us can do is commit ourselves to sharing space with better versions of ourselves as often as we can.

The stories we use to determine our meaning and/or worth are indeed a part of the legacies we leave behind because they inform who and what we care about. The stories we live in inform our hopes and aspirations about who and what we can be in the world and how we are compelled to align our actions with what we believe. Certainly, the possibilities of what we can be are only limited by the worth we assign to what we see in the mirror and the efforts we contribute to discovering the best version of ourselves. Connecting the stories we are living to the legacies we leave behind is an important element of seeing ourselves worthy. However, we are never excused from the responsibility of owning the space we occupy, none among us is without regrets, bad decisions or unutilized wisdom but each of is required to try to do and be better anyway. The legacy of that effort and the possibilities it offers should inspire each of us to use the time we have to do the things we think are important. In the end our legacies are not just who we are or were not, but also who or what we intended to be. Our legacies and the possibilities they offer are ultimately bound by our execution and less by objective.

V.

THE CONNECTION BETWEEN IDENTITY DEVELOPMENT, EDUCATION AND EXISTENTIAL THREATS?

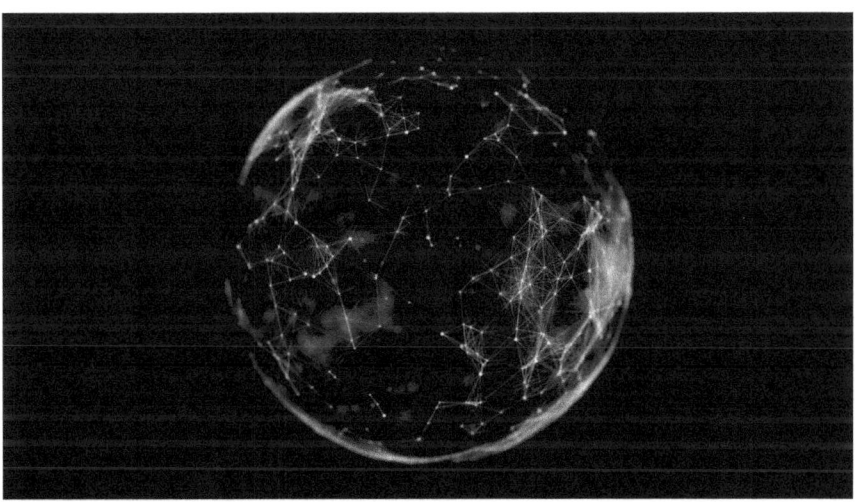

Identity development and education what's the connection?

E ducation in its broadest sense is the cultural transmission of information that explains why the world is the way it is. It attempts to explain social interactions and otherwise, history, natural phenomenon, understandings, beliefs, logic, and ways of being. It directly and indirectly imparts values, informs perspectives, and provides justifications for happenings in the world we perceive. More importantly, education in its most applicable aspects provides; thought models, navigational routes (socially, spiritually, emotionally, and of course physically) that help aid in the survival of both societies and individuals. One's educational experiences are intimately related to the stories we develop to explain our worth to ourselves and to the world we contend.

The transmission of information used to explain the world is not confined to a single source, rather it is a process that involves a coordinated collection of information streams that serve to support the survival of communities, institutions, ideas, and perceptions of reality. All of which in varying degrees provide the foundation for the stories we construct to explain the meaning we have to ourselves and to the world to which we wish to respond. The imprint of our educational experiences on the stories we tell ourselves is persistent, but they are also malleable if we are willing to do the work that allows us to challenge our own perceptions and beliefs; no small task in any regard for understanding who we are and why we matter.

The connection between identity development and education is both implicit and explicit in terms of the relevant information streams used to make sense of the worth we construct for ourselves. Explicit in the sense that schools, families and spiritual frames of reference all seek to address fundamental questions of identity. Each of these kinds of information streams attempt to inform, influence and shape the way individuals and communities understand who they are. Moreover, these and other information streams like them often work to deliberately construct paths of meaning that guide individuals, groups and communities to understand their sense of worth in particular ways. These information streams and the kinds of organizations that produce them encourage a process of identity development that shapes not only what is seen in the mirror but also the perception of institutional outcomes. They attempt to frame acceptable responses to unjust outcomes, the scope of imaginations and dreams, but more importantly they often explicitly seek to encourage an identity development process that maintains both their relevance and influence on individual and collective decision-making processes.

Implicit because the cultural transmission of information that informs our sense of self and the world we perceive is never ending and frequently unannounced. They are often embedded in interactions and dynamics that are rewarded or punished. They are implicit because the rewards and punishments are not formal and rarely are they result of predetermined results, rather they are often seemingly unimportant social dynamics that provide permissions and prohibitions that reinforce a broader structure that sometimes seems invisible; but it is always transmitting information that serves to explain acceptable versions of identity development that too often ensure results that are not in the interests of the actors unless they serve a broader function that works to support a status quo.

The connection between education and identity development is embedded in the necessity to construct a version of reality that can be collectively understood and navigated. The stories we construct to explain the paths we forge for ourselves cannot be easily separated from the information garnered from our educational experiences. In fact, our educational experiences often serve as the foundation of the stories we construct to explain our worth to ourselves and to others. If each of us is a uniquely woven quilt, one of the fabrics used by all of us is the information we collect from our educational experiences. Some may use more or less fabric and certainly each of us develops our own unique patterns with the materials we use but nonetheless the two are intertwined in ways that are often inextricable. We use the information from our educational experiences to help make sense of the chaos we call life and what we perceive as potential dangers and challenges.

Education and existential threats

The idea of existential threats is closely related to the stories we used to explain; why the world is the way it is, how it ought to be and how we fit in it. When we develop stories that establish our presence in the world, it is natural to concern ourselves with the things we believe might threaten it. In short, an existential threat refers to anything that disrupts the version of reality that we believe provides us with a sense of purpose or meaning. An existential threat in part disrupts the stories that connect what we see to what we believe. The meanings we make of these connections are both simple and complex, sometimes they are rooted in an external reality but often they are not. In essence the construction of existential threats represents the deepest seeded fears of both individuals and communities.

Education provides what appears to be reliable data to explain the threats we perceive and the magnitude of their impact on life as we imagine it. Existential threats as we understand them are those possibilities that require us to reorder the world in a way that is not just unfamiliar but one in which our value is compromised. Our Educational experience among other things provides each of us with a sense of truth, normalcy, and acceptability. They don't just provide the foundation for the stories we construct, oftentimes our educational experiences serve as the primary authors. They often inform us as to who we are like and who we are not alike, they aid us in constructing what is in our interest and what is not. They don't just tell us what something is, they often explain why it is so.

Our educational experiences, in whatever manner they present themselves, have the expressed intent to frame what we should think is important and what we should do about it. Existential threats are those challenges that are important, disrupt our stories, and ultimately test our sense of self value in fundamental ways. Our educational experiences are often, if not always, deliberately designed to frame the things that meet those criteria, for both individuals and communities simultaneously. Our educational experiences too often imprint on us the interests of those who are the sources of information, but rarely do they compel us to do the work necessary to examine our meaning making processes for ourselves. In that condition there is the danger of constructing existential threats that are not rooted in our own stories but in the stories of people who either do not know us or even worse have little concern for what we believe is in our interests.

The role of our educational experiences in the construction of what we believe are existential threats is dangerous, inextricable, and vitally important. Dangerous in the sense that when an existential threat is not rooted in the understanding one has for their own sense of worth it can be manipulated for the interests of others. Inextricable in the sense that even when we reject the acceptance of the threats offered by our education experiences, each of is required to do the work to understand "why" and that often compels more examination of our educational experiences and what they mean. Important in the sense that few things are more important than understanding one's sense of worth and what challenges it. When our educational experiences are disconnected from the stories we live, they invite us to live another story that amounts to little more than collective delusions.

Education vs. collective delusions

The distinction between collective delusions and education may be less discernible than at face value. Collective delusions are in essence shared fears and concerns that challenge or disrupt a version of reality. Education to the contrary is purported to be an academic and scientific investigation of the world in way that helps us make sense of it. While the facts and information we are exposed to in educational spaces are rarely presented as a version of reality, indeed much of what we call education is more like an agreed upon collective delusions. While our education process is generally understood as an objective endeavor that helps us to understand and process the happenings of the world.

Collective delusions are complicated in that they rarely require much in the way of external validation. Delusions are things that are false, even when they are filled with factoids that may or may not be true nonetheless, they are generally thought to be truthful. The education process is not one specific place and time; it is all the information we take in from the beginning to the end of our lives that we use to make sense of the stories we are living and also giving support to understanding the stories of "others." Collective delusions are born from a series of systemic interactions between people and social structures. When people believe in a potential outcome of a situation even if it is not true and they make what they believe are moves to prevent a particular version of reality from coming into existence. Collective delusions often feel like eduction because the false narratives are repeated with frequency and authority. While collective delusions are not education, they are often a crucial part of any given society, sometimes they help, but collective delusions are never true even when they are useful.

Education on the other hand is not something that is clearly distinguishable from collective delusion. While education is a cultural transmission of knowledge, attitudes and skills about how the world works, it also serves as the foundation for our individual and collective worth. Education is a process of studying the world both practically and analytically for the purpose of improving both our understanding about the world and our place in it. The line between collective delusion and education is particularly complicated because they both inform who we think we are and the worth we think we have to ourselves as well as to the world. Education differs from collective delusion in one important way, the usefulness of an education process is predicated on the sense we think we have as individuals while collective delusions have no such requirement they don't have to benefit us, we just need to believe they do.

Education the ultimate storyteller

While our educational experiences tend to have a significant impact on the stories we choose to live, there should be no misunderstanding that collective delusions are much more the rule than they are the exception. Both education and collective delusions rely on our analyses about our wonders related to those parts of the lived experience that are not easily explained. Where educational stories claim to lean on information and perspectives that are ground in historical and scientific methodology, collective delusions tend to rely on sub position, fear, anger, and other non-scientific sources. There are those among us who make a clear distinction between which is delusion, and which is education. However, often when we investigate further, we often find as many similarities as we do differences.

There is no question about the destructive nature of collective delusions in part because their existence often contradicts validated historical and scientific information. While the contradiction alone is not determined to be a decisive event itself, it should and does highlight all the red flags necessary to intensify our critique of the knowledge production process. Frequently, intensifying the scrutiny of the data collection process reveals a circumstance as education or collective delusion but not 100 percent of the time. Often these analyses unearth complicated facts that make a clear determination as one or the other difficult if not near impossible.

In the end collective delusions require verified observations, analyses and experiences to remain unknown or at least undetermined, and time does not make false things true, nor does it make true things false. So, it is true that collective delusions are often a central part of any society's reality, time is often their most dangerous foe. Time is the friend of a truth searching process and often places in peril the longevity of collective delusions. Consequently, education tends to be the ultimate storyteller but only for those who choose it over collective delusion. There are those among us who would willingly accept a comfortable falsehood over a complex, tense, and verifiable reality. Moreover, we should never anticipate a time when those who would make that choice is not among us. While education in the end will generally be the ultimate storyteller, it will also always be the result of the conflict that occurs when different versions of reality are occupying the same place at the same time.

VI

THE IMPACT OF RACE ON IDENTITY DEVELOPMENT, THREAT PERCEPTION AND CALCULATING HUMAN WORTH

Race and identity development

The identity development process of all human beings is both informed by and intersects with their understanding of the groups to which they believe they belong. Few things impact the identity development process more comprehensively than race. Race, almost unlike any other physical feature, has a unique and comprehensive ability to modify the entire lived experience of an individual. It has an impact on the likelihood of an infant or mother surviving the birth process, it impacts on the quality of school experiences of young people, the possibility of experiencing and surviving police and community violence, and moreover the presence and perception of race shades overall life expectancy of an individual and community to include access quality health care. The role race plays in the identity development process is nearly incalculable because of the totality of its effect on human experience.

While it is still altogether unclear exactly what race is, there can be no doubt about the effects of its perception. The stories people tell themselves to explain, ignore, apologize, codify, justify, resent or resist the implications of racial identities are as varied as there are people. Race often requires individuals and communities to develop stories that explain its place in their individual lives and more broadly in the world in which they perceive. The role race plays in identity development is difficult to assess because the mechanisms to assign it to change over time and are continuously impacted by while simultaneously shaping the lenses we use to understand it. The social, political, legal, psychological, spiritual and even ideological implications of race and its impact on the imagination of an individual, community, organization, and nation can be profound.

The quest to understand the world we perceive and ourselves in is nearly impossible to do without some account for the perception of race. Race aligns itself to the compulsion to understand ourselves in ways that are both dangerous and comforting. Dangerous in the sense that race informs us of our desire to assign worth to ourselves and others based on little more than common delusions and often misunderstood social cues, but comforting in the sense that it appears to provide useful logic to human dynamics both in our own minds and in the world, we wish to understand. In addition, race informs us how we navigate dangers, understand outcomes, make social and political decisions in circumstances that are not always clearly rational. If identity development is in part a mechanism to promote survival, race is an indispensable tool, lens, or modus operandi. The perception of race in the understanding of threats both individual and systemic can sometime mean the difference between life and death. More to the point, race appears to be a critical factor in the calculation of human worth in ways that are particular and specific to a circumstance while also in the broadest possible sense at the same time. Negotiating that dynamic is no small matter and the magnitude of the stakes are difficult to overestimate.

Race and the calculation of Human worth

The notion of human worth has within it tensions that are not easily resolved. The tension is housed in the contradiction that human worth is in some ways priceless, suggesting every human life is precious and irreplaceable; juxtaposed with the apparent acceptable institutional disparities that impact different groups in very different ways with race and ethnicity often serving as key indicators. Certainly, race is not unique in this dynamic, there are other categories of humanity that appear to have a significant impact on an individual's lived experiences such as gender identity, sexual orientation, religious affiliation, ethnicity and others. None of these are without significant consideration in the journey to understand "who we are" and "why we matter." However, within each of those categories it is important to examine the impact of race and the ways it complicates, supports and shades the lived experiences of individuals, families, and groups in ways that are uneven both generally and in particular circumstances. It is for that reason that race as a factor should be examined distinctively for its impact on the stories, we tell ourselves about why the world works the way we perceive it.

As one attempts to make meaning of their existence, it is nearly impossible to say with any certainty how the factors that impact our identity are assed in our own minds. Nonetheless, each of us is required to explore our worth in ways that help us understand ourselves and the space we occupy. In that endeavor race is a crucial player because while it is a significant factor in what we see in ourselves, it often frames how other people perceive us and it looms large over the meaning of social interactions both within and between racial communities. This phenomenon is further complicated by the absence of a shared meaning or collective understanding of the concept of race. For some races it is little more than skin pigmentation, but for others race is much more than that. It is perceived to impact individual and collective perceptions, culture, biology, political realities, legal contexts, mate selection, family values, and the list seems to be endless. The question remains: how do we approach an idea like human worth and account for the presence of race?

Human worth cannot simply be understood or evaluated by presence of spoken or written words, human worth is grounded in the interactions of human beings, the outcomes of our social institutions and policies, and ultimately by the amount of human injustice that is tolerated by individuals, communities, and institutions. The impact of race and ethnicity on the tolerance of injustice provides some insight into how human worth is calculated. Of course, no one with certainty can say what the worth of any individual may be, but we can arrive at reasonable estimations based on how individuals and systemic structures deal with perceived differences of people in different racial categories. There can be no doubt that the impact of no whiteness as a conceptualized racial space seems to play a significant role in the way certain humans are perceived, processed, and understood. The question of race and human worth is certainly not without potential conflict, tension, disagreement, and some degree of collective delusion. While race itself may be the result of a collective delusion, the impact of its perceived effects on the lived experiences of individuals and groups is undeniable.

The stories each of us lives and constructs are often used to explain the relationship between race and human worth. However, no objective analysis of the impact of race on the lived experiences of individuals can suggest that it is a positive factor for people who belong to the not white category. The impact of collective delusion on understandings of race is nearly impossible to factor out, given that the concept of race was born out of collective delusions, fears, and control. None of which are rooted in educational information streams or are they? While each of us has to grapple with our understanding of race and its historical relationship with institutional outcomes. However, any understanding of race has to account for the element of individual decision making, on some level each of us is making decisions about our worth through the stories that we are choosing to live. Our stories are not only evidence of the worth we assign to ourselves but value we assign to others when all the information we have about them is the racial group they are perceived to belong. A central reason race and human worth have a complex relationship is because even people within the same racial category are living different stories and sometimes the stories they are living contradict one another.

However, even in the nonwhite categories of racial identity the variation of stories being lived is difficult to determine. There seems to be even among nonwhite racial categories negatives distinctions among themselves about human worthiness. This challenge is further complicated by the fact that even among white racial categories there are distinctions and social hierarchies that are not easily explained. All of which should play some role in our understanding of the relationship between race and the calculation of human worth. The connection between race and human worth is probably housed more in collective delusions, but nonetheless each of our stories has to contend with facts we think we understand, the worth we assign ourselves, the groups to which we believe we belong and the perception of the world we believe we live in.

Race and threat perception

Race can in one circumstance be seen as a strength and in another be perceived as vulnerability. Each of us must calibrate our perception of race to our understanding of how we believe it impacts on our ability to live the stories that help explain our place in the world. As we are constantly adjusting, denying or constructing the stories that help us understand our worth, race for some presents elements for which must be accounted. For others it is something that rarely plays a significant role in understanding who we are and why we matter.

Threats are conceptualizations of elements that challenge our story, our value in our story, or that conflict with how we understand the happenings in the world we perceive. Too often when we are seeking understanding about threat perception our unit of analyses are too narrow in part because our comprehension window tends to be smaller than the reality it seeks to explain. Sometimes the stories we are living appear to be simple but that is almost never the case. As the impact of race contributes to the threats we perceive to our stories, it is also important to contextualize the relationship race has with other important aspects of our identity such as gender, sexual orientation, religion, sex, lived experiences, and any other meaningful element that informs what we see when we look in the mirror.

Threat perception almost never happens in a vacuum, it is almost always informed by what we see in the mirror and what we think we understand about the world. It is also impacted by our view of the threat perceptions of those around us. Understanding the process to calculate threats or being aware of the contributing factors that invite us to perceive threats reveal elements of our identity to ourselves that are often unavailable to us at other times. When we seek to understand what threatens others and why, we are empowered to better understand our own and what they mean to our sense of meaning and value. Threat perceptions are not simply relevant to a particular identity or story; they are often informed by the impact we believe it has on the groups that we believe include us. When the groups we belong to are perceived to be threatened invariably it is in our interest to understand the effect such circumstances have on us and the people we care about.

When race is believed to be a factor in the understanding of threats and their meanings, they are often absorbed as existential in nature.

Not just posing a risk to our individual stories but to all the stories we understand to be familiar. Under such circumstances the permission perceived to defend the lives we wish to live are far more drastic and dangerous. They are sometimes born out of irrational fears, but not always. How does one respond rationally to a phenomenon that they believe challenges the world as they understand it? Even more complex, when the fear is based on a perceived vulnerability that by all accounts is not "real" but the effects of it are clearly measurable and identifiable. The connection between race and threat perception is both fascinating and terrifying. The amount of disruption perceived is often in direct proportion to the amount of disruption that is permitted to be inflicted. The result can and has been devastating to entire communities.

The potential dangers from such connections, understandings and possibilities should never be underestimated. They have been the source of the most destructive conflicts in human history. When race and threat perception inform our stories, they often can activate the darkest aspect of our identity and provide permission to visit unimaginable horror on those who are perceived to disrupt the world we are determined to imagine. It is an ominous reminder to each of us about why it is important to understand not just the stories we tell ourselves but why it is important for each of us to give some attention to the stories of those around us. The stories that help explain our place in the world are powerful, they connect us to some and divide us from others, in ways that are predictable and ways that are not. The role race plays to the stories that we live is a varied as the anything else that we construct in the mirror, however few things are as tumultuous to our psyche, to our understanding of our experiences, to our life expectancy, our physical safety, our social relationships, our perceived worth or anything else of value to what we think we mean and why it matters.

The connection between the perception of race, the stories we live that help explain our worth and the development of threats that we believe pose a risk to our stories and the stories of those we find similar is worthy of exploration. The intersection of those spaces requires a dance of caution, concern, fear, perception, preparation, possibility and the defense of life as it is understood by our sense of meaning. In addition, the effort demands the ability to maneuver those elements in ways that support the effort to defend our existence as we understand it. It necessitates managing fears, vulnerabilities and aspirations, they together represent the essence of a political reality that is rooted in understanding both stories and interests of friends and foes alike.

VII.

THE POLITICS OF THE STORIES WE LIVE

Storytelling and politics twin functions?

One of the many reasons we develop stories to explain our worth is to order and conceptualize the world in such a way that our stories help us to determine our interests. The relevance of these interests to others varies both to individuals and groups. As we go about the business of living out our stories, the journey forces us to determine who our allies are and who represents a potential disruption to our story or stories (a threat). Our stories often mandate that we examine and re-examine the resources available to us to create physical, mental, emotional, and other kinds of support for our stories and the stories that make sense to us.

The stories we tell ourselves about our meaning are critical to how we understand our interests. They often invite us to assess an environment for allies, support, and dangers. Politics require the same evaluation of an environment for almost the same reasons. As each of us lives out our stories there are those among us who have more resources available to both support their stories and sustain meaning for their presence in the world they understand. The employment of those resources to influence others to share the same concept of the world, or on a particular issue, or a set of issues, is heavily influenced by one's ability to both understand your story and determine where and how there are actual or perceived connections to the interests they wish to promote.

One consequence of the substantial number of stories that are present at any given moment, there has to be a determining factor on whose story will drive the allocation of collective resources. In the same way our stories compel us to determine friends, foes, and otherwise so does a political process. A political perspective is simply a portion of the story or stories one is living. Our stories have within them our interests, what supports it and what does not; so, does our political perspectives. One could easily make the argument that living out our stories is a political process, and a political process determines whose stories are told and for what purpose (interests). The purpose of the story or political perspective is never irrelevant because when the purpose is understood, one's interests can be determined.

No story exists without corresponding interests because it is the interests that provide a given story or stories the support necessary for its survival. Politics is sometimes individual stories and interests masquerading as collective stories because of the difference in resources to which each of us has access. We live our stories in part because we believe they represent our best chance of survival as we understand it. Politics in part helps us achieve the same goal. Politics is an artistic story telling process that one believes is the best route to realizing a world that matches the stories, he, she, they or them wish to contend.

63

Politics and the stories we live in serve twin functions in the sense that each seeks to present a version of reality that matches the story to be understood as in an individual or group's interest. When groups are influenced to incorporate elements into their stories, the compelling and connecting forces are often driven by a shared fear, concern, or vulnerability; as such it frequently creates a fertile environment for collective delusions to take hold. When collective delusions serve political interests and receive support that invite people to share them, they are very difficult if not near impossible to dismiss. Not because it is difficult to reveal their shortcomings, but because believing them is often understood to be in line with the interests that connects with the stories we wish to affirm. Few things impact our version of reality more than our commitment to supporting stories in our interests even when they don't represent our truth.

The differences between the stories we live in and the politics we engage in are often time negligible, because one often feeds and supports the other. The connection between politics and individual and group meaning making can be found in our shared fears or aspirations and often both. However, when we are driven by our collective fears, we are more likely to give permission to inflict harm, than when we seek to discover common aspirations. To the extent that our politics are driven by common fears is the extent we are less able to connect with our collective best selves. When our politics are driven by collective delusions, we promote the destruction of the very things we believe are helping us to survive. When ideas, perspectives, and interests are connected by collective delusions that support the stories we live and the politics we engage in; we make time and truth the enemies of our reality. Moreover, it also taints the imagination of what is possible by perceived shared collective political interests.

The art of the possible

When our stories are informed by the idea that together we can build and develop realities that are not perfect but are at least based on the notion of the common good. The notion of the common good is critical to divergent political interests. The concept of a common good requires stories that are diametrically opposed to one another to find ways to co-exist. Such an arrangement must allow for the presence of areas of tension, deep disagreement, and some comfortability and acceptance of the unknown. Our natural tendencies to anticipate danger in disagreement, fear of the unknown and the desire to support our perceived interests are impacted by our need to understand the stories and interests of others, particularly those who diverge the most from our own.

The stories we believe provide us with value and meaning in our perceived reality are both our sanctuary and nemesis. Our sanctuary because our stories tend to provide us with comfort and emotional safety. However, sometimes they are our nemesis, because when our meaning is not based in an external reality but more connected to a collective delusion. Collective delusions often decrease possibilities, and solution sets. Resulting in a diminishment of what is possible, for no other reason than mutually shared and valued realities are generally not the goal of collective delusions. Too often collective delusions activate a sense of fear and anxiety that works against the energy necessary to explore the art of the possible.

The art of the possible requires at least the willingness and awareness of a common good and a shared understanding of its implications. There should be no doubt that the stories we develop about our understanding of why we are here are an important component of our politics. Is it possible to develop stories that invite us to see our connections to the stories most unfamiliar to us? The art of the possible is grounded in the notion of seeing connections where others see divergence. Can individual safety criteria be accomplished through collective aspiration? In part the answer to the question is rooted in our sense of being, the question is: does or can that change over time? Of course, the answer to the question is yes, it can change overtime, and it often does. A quintessential element to the discussions about our stories and the identities they inspire is, can the stories we live invite us to explore what it means to operate with a shared common good. None among us can decide for anyone else but the result must be a sense of individual value that is rooted in a shared collective efficacy.

Our political processes tend to force an investment in one story or another, often at the expense of another version of reality. It is what most of us call winning. Can we develop a version of political winning that compels each of us to understand the suffering of people who do not share our story? Moreover, can we develop a version of winning that imparts consideration and reflection on every member of the process. Forcing each of us to confront questions like: What are the blind spots in my story? What are the differences in the stories of those most unfamiliar to us? These and other questions like them are the beginning of an awareness of the art of the possible. However, in our political pursuits just because we want something that does not mean we should have it. How do we evaluate the demands each of us place on our political process? Are we pursuing what we think is the best path for our collective or are we simply working to achieve our political goals with little concern for the impact it may have on others. When we seek to have our interests prevail as a primary goal, our desire to achieve political ends is little more than gratification, pleasure seeking for its own end.

Gratification by any other name

Desire and politics are complex bedfellows, while desire is housed in a longing to have something happen, politics requires an effort and assessment to realize a goal and the ability to determine if it has been accomplished. When desire and politics are inappropriately intertwined it invites a pursuit of political agendas that may or may not be effective law and policy, but they are nonetheless advanced by individuals and groups who feel compelled to achieve them regardless of impact and effect. Consequently, the achievement of political goals that are filtered through a conceptual framework that accounts for the notion of the common good or an awareness of the impact that goal has on the stories' others are living is an important element of a healthy political process. When a political process allows and even encourages desire to serve as philosophical foundation for the political agendas the entire system is in peril.

The presence of desire in politics is probably an inevitability, that is why it is important that any political process and/or agenda have a sense of the impact it has on people who are living different realities. Every successful political agenda that is rooted in desire almost always quiets some element of the world that is often ignored when it is best to listen. The danger in having desire plays a significant role in the political process is that there those among us with more access to resources that allow them to realize more political success than those with less resources. When people have access to an abundance of political resources their desires often masquerade as collective policy. When we are seeking political ends simply because we want them but give no attention to the impact it would have overall that is simply gratification by another name.

In competitive theaters winning often has its own reward, moreover, winning to some justifies whatever is necessary to bring about the desired outcome. When political agendas are fueled by desire their realization often causes more problems than they solve. In part because they were often never connected to the interests of the stories of too many people. When the ability of individuals to impact the political process is skewed heavily to the privileged their desires are often applicable to people who share stories of favor which most people do not. Interestingly enough too often people can be convinced that supporting efforts that are not in their interest can somehow support their stories. In such cases desire is a significant factor because it takes on its own importance. Too often People want to achieve political successes that are housed in collective delusions with little connection to realizing outcomes that are in any way related to a shared common good or any awareness of the impact the result may have on people living different stories. A reality that leads to more people who either don't trust the process or believe the process itself is not in their interest.

When desire and gratification are the driving forces of a political process the systemic ability of politics to do good for most people is severely compromised. In addition, when people win, they are not invited to have any concern for the wholistic impact of their success on the collective. When people realize success in that way, it encourages others to make similar efforts to realize their goals. Making desire and gratification foundation of political legitimacy. As a result, less stories are accounted for in the outcomes of political competitions and consequently infusing everything that is necessary for the destruction of the system in its entirety. Often providing each of us with living stories that are not accounted for with all the reasons we need to either further corrupt the system or completely disregarded its veracity all together.

Can we save ourselves from us?

The vicious cycle that often results from desire and gratification is not beyond our ability change, but we often do need a compelling reason to be reflective about our contribution to a compromised process. Every success realized in a process that disregards the stories of most people brings us closer to a system wide breakdown. Forcing a face-off between achieving our political desires and developing political exercises that do the best for most people. We have to confront our gratification efforts with what is healthy for the collective. Each of our stories has been uniquely designed to further both our survival and our interests. There is no natural process that encourages us to understand how getting what we want may not be in our ultimate interest, especially when we perceive getting what we want to be in line with our survival and our political interests.

The stories we live develop about our sense of meaning are not collective efforts, while they do have collective implications because they play out in our public spaces. They are constructed from subjective and individualized pursuits and interests. Furthermore, they are built out of rational and irrational understandings of what we think it means to be who and what we are. Which often impacts the ability of any one of us to clearly communicate to someone outside our bodies what it means to be us. As a consequence, everything that is necessary for us to stave off perceived impending dangers contradicts the intent of that process because it requires us to enhance potential dangers, create more unknowns, and cooperate with perceived foes or enemies. All things that are our stories are designed to minimize and when possible, eliminate. Saving ourselves requires each of us to engage in activities that we otherwise naturally want to avoid.

If we are to save ourselves from us, we are required to be willing to potentially lose more political contests, understand unfamiliar stories, and commit to understanding and operating with a notion of a common good. It would be very difficult for most to do any one of those things, and it is nearly impossible to do all of them simultaneously without an exceptionally compelling reason. An important question that must be confronted is: does our own survival constitute the reason we need? While the answer remains to be seen, the potential negative outcomes should be unbearable for us all. Each of us will be required to see something more important than our own individual meaning as the prize and that remains as the fundamental threat to each of our stories as we understand them.

Each of us would have to conceptualize an understanding of our worth that includes some awareness of people living stories that are both diametrically opposed to our own and some consideration for stories of people who are generally unfamiliar to us. How each of us arrives at a place that allows our stories to incorporate activities that are not completely grounded in our particular interests is as daunting as it is complex. However, it is not a choice in the larger sense of our interests, it would appear that all our stories are in some way affected by the decisions that each of us makes. Why we do so is up to each of us but the impact of us not doing so will drive the future that we all experience.

VII.

The Presence Of The Most High In The Stories We Live And The Response To Existential Threats

O ver 90% of humans have some understanding of a supernatural force operating in existence that is beyond human control, and some would say beyond human understanding. The range of beliefs that constitute those understandings of a metaphysical presence are deeply divergent. Frequently, our individual senses of worth are informed by belief structures that are oftentimes believed to be wholly unassociated and dissimilar from one another. As a result, deeply held fears that are sometimes nearly impossible to clearly articulate and are often poorly understood serve as barriers that sometimes seem insurmountable in the effort to understand another person's or group's story.

The relevance of the role of spirit to the development of our worth is critical to understand even for that portion of a collective who does not subscribe to the notion. Usually when one does not believe in the presence of a Most High it is for reasons that are just as subjective as the reasons for people who do, often with very similar levels of passionate beliefs. The understanding of threats under these contexts is at best complex and at worst existential. The role or presence of a Most High in the stories we construct and the meaning we get from them is relevant even in stories that reject the idea because they nonetheless must contend with its presence in their life.

The extent to which the stories we live are informed by a Divine origin, there is often less opportunity to realize any compromise to the understanding of the covenant one believes they have with their maker. Moreover, any phenomenon that in any way appears to violate what is recognized as the meaning of that agreement is often met with significant force emotional, spiritual, physical or otherwise. The effort to both explains and expresses human worth is embedded in the stories we tell ourselves that help give our existence meaning.

The presence of a Most High often serves as a cohesive element that helps our stories to respond to the unknown. When our stories are interrupted by a force that disrupts what we believe to be our relationship with our maker, there is a tendency to understand that as a threat to existence as we understand it. While every story we live has to answer fundamental questions about why we exist, the role of a Most High provides clarity while introducing incredible complexity. The clarity and complexity are both important elements in the effort to understand our stories and the stories of others.

To whom or to what do we belong?

To whom or to what do we belong remains a quintessential question about matters related to the spirit. Are we the result of scientific inevitability or the outcome of a Divine design. Questions like those have compelled unbounded searches for the meanings we have for our existence. Our understanding of a Most High and the parameters that apply that understanding to our lives and the decisions we make is often crucial to the construction of the stories we live. In part because the answers to such critical questions provide permission for our response to any challenge we experience in our life. How do we apply concepts like grace, humility, passion, perseverance, anger, gratitude, love, obedience and retribution? It appears that these concepts and others collectively contribute to the understanding that each of us has about to whom or to what do we belong?

The question in essence seeks to create parameters for the range of responses that can be considered at any given moment no matter the circumstances. The deep personal nature of any spiritual relationship must be tested against a framework outside of any of our imagination. The question: to whom or to what do we belong? Provides a general framework of operation for all individuals that share a similar Divine origin, at least in theory. However, the stories we live, and construct tend to be very intuitive with connections and relationships that only make sense in the context of a particular lived experience. Consequently, the range of spiritual tools and concepts available to any individual are consumed in proportions that match other aspects of our story. The available tools and concepts can be applied in any configuration, proportion, and/or order that one determines necessary. Consequently, two individuals who claim to share a similar Divine origin can have divergent understandings of the question to whom or to what do they belong.

Not only can people who have similar Divine origins have different answers to the question: to whom or to what do I belong? They can also have different understandings of what the question itself means. Does the question refer to a collective spiritual source? Or does it relate to our behavior and our understanding of our mission in this life. Or does it refer to an implicit rightful place that must occupied or a statement that must be made. The spiritual domain is full of connections, complexities and concepts that are not easily reconciled and fraught with the insertion of each of our insecurities, vulnerabilities, conceits, and desires.

To whom or to what do we belong is a question that is often understood with a shared understanding. It might serve us well to explore questions of this magnitude with more scrutiny because the individual and collective stories we are living can invite us to have very different understandings of what the question means and how it applies to any moment in our lives. Moreover, it is critically important to understand that the personal nature of spiritual relationships provides space for each of us or groups of us to apply this question in any way that we think serves our interests and our story, and too often those operate as the same thing.

From where did we come; to where are we going?

Understanding and accounting for a spiritual element, that for many helps provide meaning and worth to the stories they live, is no small matter. What role and/or impact does concepts like birth and death have in a spiritual existence. In many spiritual understandings there is a sense that it is from the dirt we came and to the dirt that we must return. Sentiments like this help provide a proverbial spiritual cycle with predictability, it helps insert something believed to be known into a process that is inherently unknowable. While our capacity to understand all the things that can be known about our existence is incredibly limited, that in no way dims our desire to know or understand. As a consequence, our spiritual lenses have to in part explain things that we don't understand. The concept of death has confronted human life from the very beginning. It is that fear, vulnerability, and/or anxiety that made it necessary for us to wonder: from where did we come; to where are we going?

Death is something that is often thought of as the end of something, but what indeed if it is the beginning of the something else. The phrase, from where did we come; to where are we going, spiritually invites each of us to re-imagine the role of death on our spiritual trek. It in many ways invites us to anticipate the continuance of existence that cannot be fully understood while we yet let breathe in this life and reality. While there are those who understand their origin as part of a Devine plan, and as a result that understanding often includes restraints and obligations to living this life if we are to return to the source. However, there are those who believe that we come from nothing and will return to nothing and under that framework, one is granted much more leeway to diverge any time one determines it to be required. The latter should in no way suggest that absence of a spiritual origin is the one that lacks moral or philosophical sense of right and wrong. There is no doubt that there is a possibility of that reality, but practically many people who do not believe in a unified Devine source often have fairly well-developed systems of morality and honor.

To what and to whom do we belong invites serious consideration to fundamental questions of the unknown (spiritual or otherwise). Often when we believe we understand our meaning spiritually or in other metaphysical ways we are prepared to identify the sacred (vitally important and respectfully recognized) and the blasphemous (ultimate disrespect: particularly to something Holy or held in high esteem). The concepts and understanding we utilize to identify the two often serve as the basis for a connection or a conflict. Whatever we consider to be scared or blasphemy in our story is often informed by the question of what or whom do we belong? An everlasting uncertainty that persists is how those areas get navigated by people who are living with completely different stories that sometimes contradict one another? To that question there is no easy answer, to the point that its query has been the source of war, destruction and deep personal and interpersonal conflict. Navigating the sacred and the blasphemous has served as one of the tensest areas of human activity and spiritual application. The implications of the sacred and blasphemy seem to extend beyond this profoundly important question.

Sacred, blasphemy, or none of the above

The stories we develop and construct spiritually and otherwise pilot us on the journey we call our lives serve as mechanisms to support everyone's need to make meaning of the life they live and provide the framework to make decisions as a result. In that endeavor it is practical to identify parameters and guidance. As such, concepts like sacred and blasphemous establish concrete parameters to chart courses that are congruent with the stories we live. The things we perceive as sacred serve as affirmations that one is in line with the covenant one has with their creator. To that end, blasphemy clearly serves as a concrete prohibitive marker to identify when one has gone too far and potentially displeased one's maker.

Sacred as a concept effectively affirms things that are determined to be in alignment with it. However, the impact of a concept like sacred is much broader than providing guidance to one's internal decision making, it also serves a lens to judge the alignment of others. When one's story is informing their understanding of sacred, what happens when they have to confront others with different stories. Can someone accept the violation of something held to be sacred because someone lives a different story? Questions like that can be a significant challenge in human activity, social understanding and spiritual calibration. The presence of challenges like that have resulted in significant destruction of life and property. While sacred is largely understood through the stories individuals' and groups live, their perceived relevance is often understood to apply beyond the stories that gave birth to it. In that way the concept of Sacred is not simply guidance to individual and group meaning making, it forever implicates the dangers to the story and permissions it gives to respond to things identified as blasphemy. As a result, that notion often gives permission to attack anything that is perceived as a threat or danger. The size and significance of the authorized attack is determined by the perception of the aggrieved.

Blasphemy represents similar but different concerns and considerations. Both concepts sacred and blasphemy inform and are simultaneously impacted by the stories we live, sacred is often less defined by a common story. Blasphemy is often clearer because it is often identified as a violation of a spiritual directive. To say or do something thought to be disrespectful to an existing spiritually significant idea, place or structure. While the concept of blasphemy is no less volatile than sacred, it tends to be less contested. When something is determined to be blasphemous it was often intended to be so. When acts or words are not intended to be blasphemous, they are less so if the actor declares a different intent.

Nonetheless spiritual discernment is activated by the story or stories one lives. As a result, it is nearly impossible to separate the stories we live from the spiritual aspirations to which anyone aspires. To the extent that the stories we develop form the meaning of the worth one sees in the mirror is in large part the source of what is identified as sacred and blasphemous. The relationship between the stories that help to cultivate our individual and collective identity is at best closely correlated but often indistinguishable. If the stories an individual or group lives are poured into concepts like sacred and Blasphemous then few ideas, places or structure can share a universal distinction as anything. Even when groups of people share similar stories and conclude similar meanings rarely is the outcome identical. Consequently, people who are living in similar stories can still diverge on what is scared and what it blasphemous, to the point of great conflict and destruction.

The spiritual identities that we develop as a result of beliefs, hopes, experiences, fears, and desires fill out any gaps we may have in the story or stories we live. They represent both a collective endeavor and significant individual pursuit, that are frequently informed by different versions of similar stories. Consequently, the things we identify as sacred and blasphemous are probably more the result of the way our stories interpret and understand the Will of a Most High than they are the manifestation of the Devine Will itself. The fact that each of us is living a single story that serves our survival and sometimes the survival of those who have similar stories; When we are attempting to discern the difference between sacred and blasphemy, maybe the more accurate answer is none of the above. A conclusion that is not palatable to most spiritual conceptualizations.

The Most High in me

As each of us journeys to understand on our own terms why we exist, many of us look to metaphysical sources to understand not just our individual life but also life itself. The obvious exceptions are those who do not subscribe to the existence of a supernatural being. Either way most of us are compelled to find meaning in our existence beyond the realm of our individual lives. The desire to find the meaning of our life is contained in the effort to understand and discover our individual worth. Often when we believe we are worthy, we do so because it reflects a sense of purpose that that is believed to provide value and revelation to our existence.

The revelations in our stories provide distinct moments that require us to make decisions, take action, lean into a belief and often some combination of them all. The worth one finds, encourages, discovers, or realizes as a consequence of the process often encourages an aspirational understanding of the journey, we tend to call our lives. When a sense of being is developed that seeks to make contributions, learn, experience, grow or otherwise get better, the result is frequently manifested with an imagined better version of ourselves from our own perspective. A metamorphosis that can be fueled by spiritual ingredients but not always. The reasons we engage in such transformations are less important than what we become as a result. There are those who will attribute their motivation to the existence of metaphysical energy and others who would not. Only the stories we live in provide the explanation our motivation requires.

The need to find worth is not simply a spiritual endeavor, such an act requires the participation of every aspect of our being and its relationship to the stories we live. The effort to realize the best version of ourselves in the stories we live in serves as one method to manifest growth, resilience, gratitude, hope, determination and whatever else is necessary for each of us to experience a sense of value. It is a coveted sense of value that feeds our stories what they need to make it so, if nowhere else but in our own minds. When we are encouraged to realize versions of ourselves that are less judgmental and more introspective, we invite the possibility to realize The Most high in ourselves no matter how we use our stories to explain it. It simply refers to the effort to continue to be better version of ourselves in the stories we live in the way that matters to us. To be sure, all living beings are required to defend the life they live, and the permissions of that defense are housed in the stories that explain to us: who we are? Why are we? To Whom do we belong? Where did we come from?

IX

THE STORIES WE LIVE, NAVIGATING TRUTH AND SOCIAL DYNAMICS

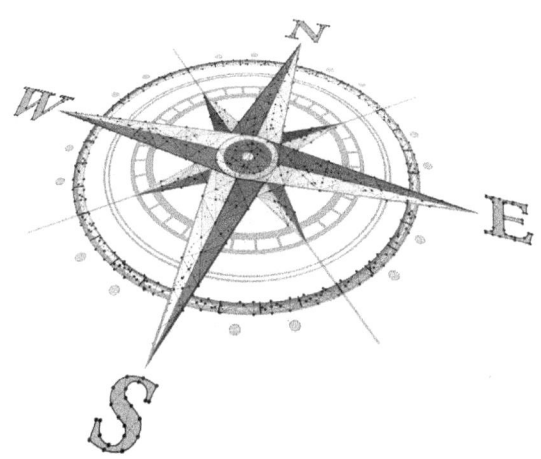

The world we understand and navigate is both informed and impacted by the stories we live. Our stories require each of us to make judgements about not only what works for us as individuals, but they provide a tool for us to understand what works for other people. The challenge is this dynamic produces an understanding that is often premised on how the story we live works for us. This injunction gives little attention to the fact that the stories we live have been explicitly designed to work for us, based on criteria we determined for ourselves. As a result, we are left to make sense of the stories we don't live and the impact of that dynamic on our understanding of our collective reality. What seems to be particularly complicated is the need to determine objective truth in an environment that is explicitly designed to not produce it.

Truth and story telling similarities and differences

Truth is a concept that requires our stories to have some overlap or at least a common perspective. When the notion of truth is contingent on the presence of a shared reality or at least a common understanding that describes a state of being, the construction of truth can be significantly implicated or implanted based on whose story is providing the framework. An important component to the truths that result, and the power and influence they reflect. Moreover, even the opposite of truth can appear to be logical, ethical and factual given the role and application of the stories it reflects or implicates. The questions that confront human activity are: how do we overcome a dynamic so fundamental that it frames what we see in our mirrors? It is without question that telling our story can be truth for any given individual.

The similarities and differences between telling our stories and telling the truth are complicated in some ways not so in others. Story telling and Truth are similar in the sense that when they are communicated with fidelity, they both reflect life and circumstance as understood from the perspective of the communicator. Different in the sense that no lived story requires validation, its value is measured internally by those who live it. However, not irrelevant is the power and influence of the storyteller, there are those who understand the stories they live to be universal, applicable and instructive to any lived experience with little to no consideration of the possibility of another story with different understandings of the truth. There are those among us who have the power and influence to convey to others what they should feel and understand about their own lived reality. This circumstance allows some people to determine the meaning and value that other people's stories should have to them as determine by people who don't not share the experience.

Whenever anyone is not the author of the stories they live, they invariably participate in collective delusions to account for the contradictions that will inevitably be produced. When anyone is living a story authored by someone else, there will be moments when interests conflict and in those moments, one has to be compelled to act against their own interest because they are making decisions that only make sense in somebody else's story. Dynamics such as these are complex because they appear often in very intimate relationships like parent to child, spouse to spouse, and between family members. This dynamic is not only relevant in external community interactions but also in the most intimate connections. How do we live our authentic stories with fidelity and speak to, address, or respond to the truths that result? It invites the question when I tell my story am I telling the truth?

When I tell my story, am I telling the truth?

The idea of idea of truth has several crucial factors; 1.) It reflects a state of being and circumstance that is tethered to an external reality that exists beyond the perspective of the particular time, the specific place, and/or the participants involved. 2.) Truth is often framed by a particular meaning, value and/or purpose that is shared across a variety of stories. 3.) The truths that are often held most dear are ones we believe to be instructive to help in the navigation of both the unknown present and future circumstances. Often as we are living our stories and collecting truths along the way, we rarely investigate with any rigor what it means to tell the truth and how that may differ from telling our story.

When we are telling our story we are thinking about, analyzing, and/or communicating how we understand our individual place in the world that we perceive. Consequently, this process is not bound by any phenomenon except our imaginations ability to rationalize and/or connect the happenings in the world both near and far from our physical being and the meaning we assign to ourselves. While all three components of truth are relevant to anyone telling their story, they are often accounted for in measurements constructed primarily to sustain those aspects of our story that we do not wish to change. Even more complicatedly sometimes our stories address things we wish we were but indeed we are not. Moreover, our stories must confront the things we wish we were not but indeed we are. Each of our stories lives this dynamic in slightly diverse ways which makes each of us unique on our own terms. However, it is possible to live a story completely disconnected from any shared reality, when done in the extreme it reflects an imbalance that often requires help to restore but that element is always present no matter how little.

The telling of our stories is a vital part of living a life of peace, self-actualization, and it is essential to develop a community that is healthy, productive, and well adjusted. The telling of our stories often adds something to the world that without it would not exist. The telling of our stories gives the world a texture, context and challenge that presents each of us and the world in general with constant opportunities to grow, change, learn, and think about things that are often in conflict with our version of reality. While there will always be a tension between telling our stories and telling the truth the tension is not often one of fidelity or integrity but sometimes it is. Sometimes the tension is not in the accuracy of the details but in the meaning of the occurrence itself. Perceived perpetrators and victims often have different understandings of the meaning and value of a particular time and space; which forces each of us to confront the question: Who is telling the truth?

While it is important to distinguish between telling our stories and telling the truth, we should do so for other purposes than to confirm accuracy and/or correctness. We should do so to provide a more thorough understanding of our own stories and what they mean to us. We should not engage in this endeavor to decide blame or demean a story that is unfamiliar. Every time that happens, we engage in a process that belittles our own story, when we find that a story is not worth telling, we put all story telling at risk. The telling of our stories is the chief mechanism for the most authentic learning that any of us can engage in. Understanding the implications of other lived stories can provide each of us with crucial insight, awareness and meaning to our own stories and how we understand our interests.

Some aspects of truth and story telling are incredibly similar. In the sense that each does rely on an assumed fidelity to authenticity. Meaning, when we are telling our stories we are explaining with an assumed integrity each of our understanding of what an idea, occurrence, or even words mean to our sense of self. More importantly, we use our story telling spaces to both understand and explain our worth to ourselves and to other people. How people react to our stories indicates and reveals how other people feel about us and the value they have for us and our stories. When our sense of self requires the diminishment of other people's stories, it reduces the value of our own because that act requires us to display the details of what it takes to reduce the importance of our own.

Truth and social dynamics point of departure

The relationship between truth and social dynamics is complicated at best. As each of us lives a story that is only visible in its entirety to us in our own minds, we live and interact in a world in which everyone is doing the same thing simultaneously. Consequently, our stories both individually and collectively are confronted by the world around us. Furthermore, there is continuous unstated uncertainty about the relationship between the notion of truth and the telling of our stories. Truth and trust in the matter requires our stories to have shared meanings that are far too often unstated. This is an important point for consideration, while truth as indicated earlier often necessitates a shared understanding of reality, that is sometimes nearly impossible to arrive at and under those circumstances, how to live together working toward shared goals in shared realities.

Social dynamics refers to that aspect of our lived experience that mandates us to navigate terrain that is not aligned with our own sense of self and the stories we live. This dynamic is not just present in the company of strangers, it is present in family dynamics, intimate relationships, and sometimes with the person we interact with in the mirror. When the presence of institutions, historical perspectives, organizations, power, and the desire to have our essential needs met, the complications of storytelling and truth become even more tenuous. Particularly when it is believed that a particular story is masquerading as truth when indeed it is a story aligned with the power to have it distributed.

When there are disparities in the impact of the outcomes of social institutions such as families, law making bodies, service institutions and collective endeavors, those disparities to some often reveal a message about whose stories matter more. Moreover, they invite the development of divergent truths about what the disparities mean and what is necessary to resolve them, if resolution is even an option on the table. When it isn't that too, some stories reveal truths and the need to tell stories individually. It helps or reveals a process that does not work for some particularly when it appears to be at the expense of others. When that is perceived how is it understood? As story telling or the truth? The answer is often housed in the perception of the viewer. Often when people perceive a process as at their expense the benefactors often see it as story telling, but when that perception is from the recipient it is often understood as truth and reality.

It is here at this point that truth and story telling diverge, not because they are in conflict but because they serve different interests. Each lived story develops its own validation and seeks connection to the interests necessary to maintain its existence. In that pursuit each story is modified in its actuality and/or in its expression in an effort to overlap with other stories that serve and meet shared interests. This reality is forever in tension with the ever-changing understanding of our value (both individually and collectively). A dynamic relevant to any understanding of any set of circumstances. As a matter of social dynamics, variations of lived individual and collective stories require understanding and graces that most stories are not equipped to promote or assimilate.

As a result, truth and social dynamics depart not because they are categorically different, but because they serve different interests with varied abilities to have elements of the stories, they live to be shared by others either by belief or experience. The interaction of truth and social dynamics can at best be complicated, while being in most circumstances in conflict, and always in danger of being irreconcilable. The endeavor to make meaning will always be both an individual and collective pursuit and as a result the interaction of truth, story telling, social dynamics and the lived experience will forever be shaped by it.

X.

IF WE ARE THE STORIES WE LIVE, DO WE SURVIVE AS LONG AS OUR STORIES ARE TOLD?

That question returns this discussion to its beginning. What is survival? Is survival a notion that is strictly understood as a physical existence? Questions like these represent a fundamental aspect to the stories that we live and how they shape our behavior. Each of us operates with an understanding we have about survival, and we are then required to apply that understanding to the stories we live. It shapes and influences the very essence of each story, impacting our decisions both big and small. While there are no right answers to questions like these, when there is disagreement about them it tends to be extremely contentious. We are designed to survive and there are those among us who believe disagreement threatens their version of survival.

As each of us must reconcile with the sometime unsettling reality of a physical end, we are often compelled to develop a pathway that allows our story to make sense to us. Each of us sojourns the thing we call life to both realize and express our worthiness and appreciation for the life we live, if only to ourselves but often to others as well. Each of us decides for ourselves what we believe is destiny and what we believe is choice. That is a burden or responsibility we have for ourselves, because we share an eventual fate and as a consequence, each of us must determine what we think that means for ourselves, the people we care about, and anything else we determine that is important to our story.

Ain't nobody getting out of here alive

The certainty of death plays a significantly distinct role in each of our stories, and in that way gives each of us a shared experience that exist beyond any characteristic, class, race, ethnicity, power dynamic, belief, or access. The sobering reality that we are here and one day we will not physically be here is a complicated but fixed element in each of our stories. As a consequence, that reality supplies the opportunity to examine the impact that immutable facts play in each of our stories. No one of us individually or collectively understands the presence of death's existence in our lives.

However, nonetheless we are all forced to contend with what we think death means to our story and its implications to our hopes, dreams, fears, beliefs, perceptions and accompanying attitudes and behaviors. Survival represents a shared goal of all things that live but the interpretation of the that survival is limited only by the imagination that perceives it. How do the concepts of survival and death impact understandings of Love, worthiness, connection, value, growth, and any other idea or concept any one of us has about the journey we travel or our understanding about the implications of the journey of others. Divergent recognitions of survival and death force us collectively and individually to decide what works for the story or stories we live and the purpose it serves.

We tend to be clear about the purpose of survival and what it means to us and our stories, but that clarity often does not transfer to notions of death. We are forced to confront questions like; is death the end of something or the beginning of something else? In part the answer is shaped by the stories we use to inform our sense of self, but it is also often simultaneously informing those understandings as well. How do we live with the presence of death in our stories? Is it the ultimate predator that stalks us from the moment we emerge from the birth canal or is it a not-so-subtle reminder that each moment in this thing we call life is precious beyond our realization. Here again there is no right answer other than each of us not only grappling with its role in our story but also understanding the role that it plays in the stories of others. It represents a shared burden, but it is individually applied and incorporated into our story in way that makes sense to us.

What is the value of our stories when we are no longer physically here? Each of us is familiar with the story of someone who is no longer physically here that we never personally met, does that constitute a form of survival? Questions like that represent our challenge because in the end none of us are getting out of here alive. Each of us must confront what we perceive about this shared reality and apply it to both the story we want to live and its connection to the story we are living when those two things are different. In essence, it is a revelation of sorts that compels us to grapple with concepts of destiny, promise and/or choice.

Destiny, promise and/or choice

The notion of survival is complex and connected for individuals because we are often forced to address questions for which we have no truly solid answers. Consequently, the resource pool that we use to navigate this important dynamic is largely unsettled, but it is a critically important area to navigate. Navigation often requires movement even when the destination is unclear. Survival can be particularly complicated because our understanding of it is rarely fixed. Our link to survival frequently transforms over time into ways that are both rational and irrational. The impact of our evolving understanding of our story (identity) responds to the things we learn, new beliefs, experiences and any fears that we develop along along the way. When we are confronted with circumstances that challenge our story in ways that invoke considerations of the unknown we are often compelled to respond in both mind and body to questions that are often unanswerable in the moment. Those questions are often related to a loss (relationship, death, job, etc), a sickness, an opportunity, unexpected set back, and even the accomplishment of an important goal.

Each of us often looks at our hopes, dreams, fears, and aspirations to explain this circumstance to ourselves within the context of the story we live. When we are confronted with situations that we believe threaten our survival; do we understand the event as destiny, the realization of a promise, or the outcome of a choice. It is not altogether impossible to perceive the event or setting as some combination of all three. While all are in one way or another valid perceptions they do individually often have very different implications.

When we believe that the journey of our story is destined, we often have less questions about the route because it leads to an inevitable result. When we believe that our story has a result that is predetermined there is a tendency to have less concern about the impact of the journey on other people's stories. In fact, when we believe our story is destined there can be a tendency to devalue the stories of others because that which is destined by its nature has more importance than that not considered to be so. While there is no question that the presence of death is again a shared reality, but the meaning of the reality can very with almost unlimited variations. When we understand our story to be destined thus more valuable, that often provides permission to only account for other stories to the extent that they are relevant to the ones we understand. Leaving the most pressing question: When one believes their story is destined, how do they apply that idea to their attitudes and behavior especially with people who live a different story?

However, the notion of promises invites different considerations that often require the fulfillment of an obligation. The notion of a promise is distinctly different from destiny because a promise generally has an "if and then" element to it. The idea of a promise frequently suggests that one must realize certain states of being that often include ideas like trust, faith and obedience between the individual and their understanding of the Most High. As a result, under those criteria one is only assured the promise if they have fulfilled their end of the bargain. While some elements of the promise can be recognized in the lived experience, important elements of the promise are often metaphysical, to be acquired only after the transition from life to death. Those who understand their life to be conducted and guided by a promise, often have to account for the stories of others in ways that one who believes they are destined generally do not.

The notion of a promise is particularly complex because there are significant perceptual differences that people have even when they are guided by the same promise. As with all things in this life our understanding of a promise is filtered through the interest of the story or stories we are living. One of the most relevant and salient questions for the promise in this context is how one applies the meaning of the promise they understand and its impact on the story they live in context with the decisions they make consequently.

Of course, the idea of promise has embedded within it the notion of the choice because one is often required to choose to oblige oneself to the terms of the arrangement. However, it is not a decision in which there is any negotiation, the question is often direct, do you accept the covenant or not? As a result, the concept of the promise and choice are very closely related but they are not identical. In the same way that promise and destiny both tend to offer a glory that can be eternal that makes the allure of the journey almost intoxicatingly irresistible given consideration of possible alternatives. The idea of choice without the pay off of glory frequently presented in destiny and promise is far too uncertain for many stories. While the attraction of glory presented by destiny and promise are convoluted with the individual perception of what is and what is to come, the route and result are nonetheless unresolved. Unresolved in the sense that when the same promise and destiny is understood differently by people who seek the same glory but display conflicting behaviors. Under those circumstances we are left with the same questions: What does that mean? Who receives the glory? In what ways are our stories valuable and worthy? How is the story we live informed by this dynamic?

The idea of choice with less emphasis on predetermined glory may be more freeing but it often lacks the clarity of a potential promise or predetermined destiny. Despite the sirens call of glory offered by the Most High there are those who see their life/story largely because of the choices they make and whatever glory there is to be had is in the results of the decisions made. When there is more emphasis on the result than on the glory the impact and presence of other stories is often more relevant in the evaluation of the outcome. Particularly when the understood glory and the result of the decision are two different things.

As we concern ourselves with survival as we understand it, with the unmodified presence of death as an ultimate culmination, how do we respond? While it is difficult to near impossible to know with any precision how this dynamic is applicable to any specific story including our own, it is simultaneously and critically important to evaluate with any accuracy our worth and the worth we have to others. At the end of the discussion, we are faced with the same unresolved questions, but if we are reflective about the way any one of us approaches them, we can better understand the implications to the stories we live, and the stories lived by others.

The journey that is me

Each of us travels a sojourn that is uniquely our own, with shared obligations, obstacles, and goals. Each filtered through a story building process that supports and affirms the value we have for ourselves.

Forming and expanding the stories that explain our worth is a crucial element to our identity. It expands well beyond what we can see in a mirror, in fact the presence of our stories converts looking into the mirror from an act to a performance. A theatrical performance with an audience, stage, and actors all in our imagination and confirmed by a story that explains why the space we occupy is worthy.

The most important biological purpose of identity development is to provide each of us with the ability to assess danger to our unique existence with our particular vulnerabilities. It is an evaluation that only each of us can make for ourselves. Consequently, no two of our journeys are exactly the same even when we experience similar occurrences and claim similar values and objectives.

Our ability to optimize the opportunities that our stories present is enhanced as we work to not only understand who we are in our space, but also investigating why does that space matter, and importantly what we must learn and do to protect the space we occupy. The pool of data we use to discern answers to those lofty questions is both dynamic and ever changing. While the external factors are ever changing and dynamic, what makes the challenge of survival that much more complex that is who we are, and our stories change over time and sometimes significantly. When we have to respond to unknowns, the perception of the "other," our own individual growth and development with the stories we construct, it is a wonder that any of us ever succeeds, but most of us do most of the time.

It is understood consciously or not that the goal of survival always has an ultimate end that is shared by everything alive. Our most interesting question is how we live in the face of much more uncertainty than knowledge. It is precisely that reality that makes the effort to understand the journey crucial not just for each of us as individuals, families, organizations, and even nations, it is important because that which lives must be defended and protected. That defense requires an understanding of the danger it faces, by evaluating story of the others and the dangers they invite. To not be vigilant in assessing the stories we tell ourselves to explain our place in the world is to play a pivotal role in our own demise. To the extent that one develops and constructs stories that clarify one's sense of self, we build the essential tools for the defense of our existence as we understand it. This process continues until it is no longer necessary, and to be clear it is necessary for as long as there is a life to be defended......